MECHANICS-
MERCANTILE
LIBRARY.

Cupcake Cakes

An Imagine Book
Published by Charlesbridge
85 Main Street, Watertown, MA 02472
617-926-0329
www.charlesbridge.com

Created by Penn Publishing Ltd.
1 Yehuda Halevi Street, Tel Aviv, Israel 65135
www.penn.co.il
Editor-in-Chief: Rachel Penn
Edited by Shoshana Brickman
Design and layout by Michal & Dekel
Photography by Danya Weiner
Food styling by Deanna Linder

Library of Congress Cataloging-in-Publication Data

Levy, Danielle, 1983-
Cupcake cakes / by Danielle Levy ; photography by Danya Weiner.
    p. cm.
ISBN 978-1-936140-57-2 (hardcover)
1. Cake decorating. 2. Cupcakes. 3. Cookbooks. I. Title.
TX771.2.L48 2011
641.8'653--dc23
                        2011032362

2 4 6 8 10 9 7 5 3 1
Printed in China, October 2011

For information about custom editions, special sales, premium and corporate purchases,
please contact Charlesbridge Publishing at specialsales@charlesbridge.com

Cupcake Cakes

Delicious, Delightful, & Spectacular

Danielle Levy

Photography by Danya Weiner

imagine!
Publishing

Table of Contents

Ice Cream Parlor Cupcake Cake (page 34)

Introduction

My love of cupcakes started when I was a child. I used to bake with my sister on the weekends, trying out different cupcakes (we called them fairy cakes where I grew up) in different colors, themes, and decorations.

To my great delight, cupcakes have become incredibly popular over the past few years. They now take on many different personalities and can be found at so many occasions. From weddings and holidays to children's birthday parties and Sweet 16s, if there's an occasion to celebrate, there's a cupcake that's just waiting to be made for it.

Nowadays, I don't just spend my weekends making cupcakes. It's become my profession! I run a little cupcake shop in Tel Aviv called ilovecupcakes that specializes in making really special cupcakes for all sorts of occasions. Since opening my shop, I've discovered so many ways to tailor cupcakes for special events. If there is a limit to the possibilities of cupcakes, I certainly haven't found it yet!

In **Cupcake Cakes**, you'll find dozens of terrific 'cake' designs made from cupcakes, cakes and plenty of imagination. They include cupcakes of every size (you'll find giant cupcakes too!) topped with dozens of frosting and decorations. Cupcake cakes are perfect for serving at celebrations and great for making ordinary days more special.

Cupcake Cakes is divided into three main chapters: Birthdays, Special Occasions and Holidays. Of course, you can use a Birthday design to celebrate a Special Occasion or vice versa. My goal is to show you different ways of presenting cupcakes. I hope you'll experiment and use your imagination when it comes to displaying your cupcakes too. You can display your cupcakes on plates, platters, multi-tier cakes stands or tea cups. They can spell out words, create patterns, be stacked in towers or propped in ice cream cones. The design possibilities are endless so switch on your imagination, get out your oven gloves and start creating. Good luck and enjoy!

Luck 'o' the Irish Cupcake Cake (mini cupcakes) (page 39) and Salted Chocolate Cupcake Cake (regular cupcakes) (page 44)

Ingredients

With many things in life, what you get out of them depends upon what you put in. This is particularly true with cupcakes since the preparation process is so easy. You'll get fantastic results as long as you choose high-quality products for all your ingredients.

Butter

Always use real butter (not margarine). It makes a world of difference. For best results, use unsalted butter that's at room temperature.

Chocolate

Always use high-quality chocolate. If you're using dark chocolate, select a variety that contains at least 70% cocoa.

Cocoa

Use high-quality cocoa powder for all recipes. It makes for a richer more chocolatey cupcake.

Flour

Cake flour is used in most of the cupcake recipes in this book. It is made from soft wheat flour and gives cupcakes a smooth texture.

Food coloring

Don't underestimate the visual power of colored frosting on your cupcakes. All it takes is a few drops of the right food coloring and your homemade dessert becomes a work of art. Many types of food coloring are available today, including ones made with natural ingredients, so choose what you like and enjoy!

Vanilla

If you can, use real vanilla pods or pure vanilla extract. The ratio is ⅓ vanilla pod equals 1 teaspoon of vanilla extract.

Tips

Cupcake sizes

Cupcake pans and liners come in a wide variety of sizes. I've use three standard sizes to create the cupcake cakes in this book, but feel free to adjust to the sizes you have at home.

Mini Diameter 0.6 inch
Small Diameter 1 inch
Regular Diameter 2 inches

Mixing the batter

It's really important that you don't over mix the ingredients in cupcakes. In many recipes, you'll see that I recommend keeping the mixing speed at low for most of the mixing, and just speeding it up at the end to medium high or high. This keeps the mixture airy, which results in a lighter, fluffier cupcake.

Sifting

I recommend sifting flour before using it to get rid of lumps.

Storing & serving

Cupcakes without frosting can be frozen for up to one month. Cupcakes with frosting can be refrigerated in an airtight container for up to 2 days. Serve cupcakes at room temperature.

Temperature

For best results, use ingredients that are at room temperature. Not only does this make the mixing process easier, but the final product tastes better. If ingredients such as butter or eggs are too cold to begin with, this simply won't combine well.

About Frosting

Frostings are so important when it comes to cupcakes. They make them fun, indulgent, decorative and lighthearted. Even if you're an experienced baker, you may not have a lot of experience with frosting, so cupcakes are a perfect chance to get started. Here are some tips.

Frosting texture

If your frosting is too runny, thicken it by adding a bit of icing sugar. If your frosting is too thick, gradually add more milk. When thinning frosting with milk, make sure you add the milk one drop at a time, and mix thoroughly after each addition, so that the frosting doesn't suddenly become too runny.

Frosting cupcakes

Frosting cupcakes is fun. You can do it with a pastry bag, an offset spatula or a knife. If you want to pipe twirls, flowers or star shapes on your cupcake, you'll want to use a piping bag with a pastry tip (page 13). If you've never done this before, practice piping your frosting on a piece of baking paper before moving on to your cupcakes.

Frosting cakes

Frosting cakes can be a bit trickier than frosting cupcakes, since you have a larger surface to cover. First of all, you'll have to remove the cake from the cake pan, so be sure to grease the pan generously in advance so that the cake releases with ease.

Once the cake is out of the cake pan, you might notice a small hill on the top. I recommend slicing this off with a large serrated knife to create a flat surface.

Though you can use a pastry bag and tip to pipe stripes and twirls on your cake, I recommend frosting cakes with an offset spatula. These have a larger surface area than ordinary knives making it easier to create a smooth layer of frosting.

Selecting the pastry bag tip

Choose high quality tips that won't rust over time. As for the shape of the tip, that's really up to you. Here are my personal favorites:

Open star tip for making classic cupcake swirls

Closed star tip for making flower swirls

Thin round tip for making smooth circles

Wide round tip for making creating smooth buttons

Thin writing tip for writing words or numbers

How to hold a pastry bag

Holding a pastry bag takes a bit of practice so be patient. When holding the bag, make sure your hand places even pressure all around the bag so that the frosting comes out easily and smoothly. Make sure your fingers don't dig into the bag.

How much frosting to use

This is completely up to you but I usually like the frosting to be half as high as the cupcake. In other words, if the cupcake is 2 inches high, I like to top it with about 1 inch of frosting.

Writing on cupcakes

Writing is a great way to personalize your cupcakes. Here are some tips to help you get it right.

- Make sure the frosting is at room temperature
- Make the frosting a bit thinner than usual so that it flows smoothly
- Practice on baking paper before moving on to your cupcake
- Draw one line at a time of each letter

Vanilla Cupcakes

Never underestimate the beauty of simplicity.
This recipe is easy to make and fun to dress up. Serve as it is or
fold in raisins, chocolate chips, sprinkles, dried cranberries...use
your pantry and taste buds for inspiration!

Makes 12 regular cupcakes

Ingredients

1½ cups cake flour
1½ teaspoons baking powder
Pinch salt
3¼ ounces unsalted butter, room
    temperature
1 cup sugar
1 large egg
1 large egg white
1 teaspoon vanilla extract
½ cup buttermilk

1 Preheat oven to 350°F and line a cupcake pan with paper liners.

2 In a medium bowl, sift together flour, baking powder and salt.

3 In a separate bowl, beat butter and sugar at high speed until light and fluffy.

4 Reduce speed and mix in egg, egg white and vanilla extract.

5 Add flour mixture to butter mixture in 3 batches, alternating with buttermilk, and mixing on low speed after each addition. Beat at high speed for 1 minute until thoroughly combined.

6 Pour batter into cupcake liners until ⅔ full and bake for about 20 minutes or until a toothpick inserted in the center comes out clean. Set aside to cool. Serve immediately or refrigerate for up to 2 days in an airtight container.

Chocolate Cupcakes

You can make this chocolate frosting even if you don't have any chocolate in the pantry. All you need is a bit of cocoa powder!

Makes 12 regular cupcakes

Ingredients

1¼ cups cake flour

¼ cup cocoa powder

1½ teaspoons baking powder

Pinch salt

3¼ ounces unsalted butter, room
 temperature

1 cup demerara sugar

1 large egg

1 large egg white

1 teaspoon vanilla extract

½ cup buttermilk

1 Preheat oven to 350°F and line a cupcake pan with paper liners.

2 In a medium bowl, sift together flour, cocoa, baking powder and salt.

3 In a separate bowl, beat butter and sugar at high speed until light and fluffy.

4 Reduce speed and mix in egg, egg white and vanilla extract.

5 Add flour mixture to butter mixture in 3 batches, alternating with buttermilk, and mixing on low speed after each addition. Beat at high speed for 1 minute until thoroughly combined.

6 Pour batter into cupcake liners until ⅔ full and bake for about 20 minutes or until a toothpick inserted in the center comes out clean. Set aside to cool. Serve immediately or refrigerate for up to 2 days in an airtight container.

Basic Chocolate Frosting

Here's a great chocolate frosting to make, even if you don't have a single piece of chocolate in the pantry. All you need is a bit of cocoa powder!

Makes about 1½ cups

Ingredients

3 ounces unsalted butter, room temperature
2½ cups confectioners' sugar
1½ tablespoons cocoa powder
2 tablespoons milk

In the bowl of an electric mixer, beat butter, sugar, cocoa and milk at high speed for about 4 minutes, until light and fluffy.

Cream Cheese Frosting

This classic frosting recipe is rich, creamy and easy to make. It's a perfect topping for carrot or chocolate cupcakes, but don't be shy about trying it in other combinations as well.

Makes about 1½ cups

Ingredients

2 cups cream cheese
1 cup confectioners' sugar
1 teaspoon vanilla extract

In the bowl of an electric mixer, beat cream cheese, sugar and vanilla at high speed for about 4 minutes, until light and fluffy.

Vanilla Frosting

There are countless ways to top a cupcake and this recipe is a great basis for dozens of them. Replace the vanilla extract with other flavored extracts or experiment with your favorite spreads.

Makes about 1½ cups

Ingredients

3 ounces unsalted butter, room temperature
2½ cups confectioners' sugar
1 tablespoon milk
1 teaspoon vanilla extract

In the bowl of an electric mixer, beat butter, sugar, milk and vanilla extract at high speed for about 4 minutes, until light and fluffy.

Frosting Variations

Follow the Vanilla Frosting recipe on the previous page, and make the following adjustments, to create these simple variations:

Almond Frosting

Replace the vanilla extract with 1 tablespoon almond extract.

Brandy Frosting

Replace the vanilla extract with 1 tablespoon brandy extract and tint with orange food coloring.

Cherry Frosting

Replace the vanilla extract with 1 teaspoon cherry extract or 1 tablespoon cherry jam and tint with red food coloring.

Honey Frosting

Replace the vanilla extract with 1 tablespoon honey.

Jam Frosting

Replace the vanilla extract with 2 tablespoons of your favorite jam. For smooth frosting, be sure to select a smooth jam.

Lemon Frosting

Replace the vanilla extract with lemon extract and tint as desired.

Orange Frosting

Replace the vanilla extract with orange extract and tint with orange or red food coloring.

Peppermint Frosting

Replace the vanilla extract with peppermint extract and tint as desired.

Rich Chocolate Frosting

Replace the vanilla extract with ⅓ cup chocolate chips. Melt the chocolate chips in a double boiler and then set aside to cool until warm to the touch. Add a teaspoon of milk if the consistency is too thick. Fold into the whipped frosting.

Royal Icing

Drizzle this on any cupcake for an easy and elegant topping. Perfect for serving at teatime, it's light and attractive and doesn't require any oil or butter.

Ingredients

2 large egg whites
4¾ cups confectioners' sugar
Juice of 1 lemon (without pulp)
Yellow food coloring, optional

1 Place egg whites in a clean bowl and beat until stiff peaks form.

2 Reduce speed and mix in sugar then beat at high speed until glossy.

3 Add lemon juice and mix for another minute. Add a few drops of food coloring to enhance the yellow color.

Chocolate Ganâche

The flavor of this topping is directly related to the quality of chocolate you use, so be sure to choose one of high quality. It's very easy to make—and hard to resist!

Ingredients

6 ounces dark chocolate, chopped
½ cup double cream
1 teaspoon vanilla extract

1 Place chocolate in a heatproof bowl.

2 Pour cream into a small saucepan and bring just to boil. Remove cream from heat and pour over chocolate.

3 Let stand for a few minutes, and then add vanilla and stir until smooth and glossy.

Creamy Caramel

This recipe calls for muscovado sugar—a coarse and sticky brown sugar that comes from Barbados. If you can't find it at your supermarket, use dark brown sugar instead.

Ingredients

1 cup brown muscovado sugar
6 tablespoons unsalted butter, room temperature
½ cup heavy whipping cream
1 teaspoon vanilla extract

1 In a small pan, heat sugar over medium-high heat, stirring continuously with a wooden spoon until melted. Take care that it doesn't burn.

2 Stir butter into melted sugar, and then remove from heat. Mix in whipping cream and vanilla extract.

Over the Rainbow Cupcake Cake

Here's an easy dream-come-true cake—it's a rainbow on the inside and out! Make sure you don't overmix the batter after adding the food coloring so that the colors stay separated.

Makes one 8½ x 15½-inch cupcake cake

Ingredients

Cupcake

4½ cups cake flour

4½ teaspoons baking powder

Pinch salt

9¾ ounces unsalted butter, room
   temperature

3 cups sugar

3 large eggs

3 large egg whites

3 teaspoons vanilla extract

1½ cups buttermilk

Red, blue and yellow food colorings

Frosting

6 ounces white chocolate, chopped

9 ounces unsalted butter, room
   temperature

7½ cups confectioners' sugar

⅓ cup milk

3 teaspoons vanilla extract

Peach food coloring

Garnish

Rainbow sprinkles

1 cherry

Cupcakes

1 Preheat oven to 350°F and generously grease an 8½ x 15½-inch giant cupcake cake pan.

2 In a medium bowl, sift together flour, baking powder and salt.

3 In a separate bowl, beat butter and sugar at high speed until light and fluffy.

4 Reduce speed and mix in eggs, egg whites and vanilla extract.

5 Add flour mixture to butter mixture in 3 batches, alternating with buttermilk, and mixing on low speed after each addition. Beat at high speed for 1 minute until thoroughly combined.

6 Place two drops of each color at different spots on the surface of the batter. Mix with care, letting the colors remain separated.

7 Pour batter into the cupcake pan and bake for about 35 minutes or until a toothpick inserted in the center comes out clean. Set aside to cool.

Frosting

8 Melt white chocolate in the top of a double boiler, and then set aside to cool until warm to the touch.

9 In the bowl of an electric mixer, beat butter, confectioners' sugar, milk and vanilla at high speed until light and fluffy.

10 Divide frosting evenly between two bowls and tint one bowl with peach food coloring.

11 Frost the bottom cake with peach frosting and the top cake with white frosting. Put the cakes together and decorate with sprinkles and the cherry. Serve immediately or refrigerate for up to 2 days in an airtight container.

Banana Birthday Cupcake Cake

Banana cake is a favorite for so many youngsters. Dress it up on a birthday by adding chocolate chips and topping it with chocolate frosting. To make it even more special, top the frosting with gummy candies!

Makes 24 mini cupcakes

Ingredients

Cupcakes

1 cup cake flour

1½ teaspoons baking powder

Pinch salt

¼ cup unsalted butter, room temperature

1 large egg

½ cup buttermilk

½ cup mashed ripe banana

⅓ cup milk chocolate chips

Frosting

2 ounces milk chocolate

3¼ ounces unsalted butter, room temperature

2½ cups confectioners' sugar

3 tablespoons milk

Garnish

Chocolate curls

Cupcakes

1 Preheat oven to 350°F and line a cupcake pan with paper liners. In a medium bowl, sift together flour, baking powder and salt. In a separate bowl, beat butter and sugar at high speed until light and fluffy. Reduce speed and mix in egg.

2 Add flour mixture to butter mixture in three batches, alternating with buttermilk, and mixing on low speed after each addition. Beat at high speed for 1 minute until thoroughly combined. Fold in the mashed banana and chocolate chips.

3 Pour batter into cupcake liners pan until ⅔ full. Bake for about 20 minutes or a toothpick inserted in the center comes out clean. Set aside to cool.

Frosting

4 Melt chocolate in the top of a double boiler and set aside to cool until warm to the touch. In the bowl of an electric mixer, beat butter, confectioners' sugar and milk at high speed until light and fluffy. Fold in the melted chocolate. Frost the cupcakes or cake and garnish with chocolate curls. Serve immediately or refrigerate for up to 2 days in an airtight container.

Colossal Caramel Cupcake Cake

Create a mountainous cake topped with creamy homemade caramel! Perfectly served with French vanilla ice cream.

Makes 6 small cupcakes
and one 4-inch round cake

Cupcake Cake Idea

· **Cake stand**
· **Toothpicks***

Place the cake on the cake stand. Insert a toothpick halfway into the center of the cake and gently press on a cupcake. Affix the rest of the cupcakes in a similar manner on top of the cake.

* Remove toothpicks before serving.

Ingredients

Cupcakes

1½ cups cake flour
1½ teaspoons baking powder
Pinch salt
3¼ ounces unsalted butter, room
    temperature
1 cup sugar
1 large egg
1 large egg white
1 teaspoon vanilla extract
½ cup buttermilk
Creamy Caramel (page 18)
Vanilla Frosting (page 16)

1 Preheat oven to 350°F. Line a cupcake pan with paper liners and generously grease a 4-inch round cake pan.

2 In a medium bowl, sift together flour, baking powder and salt.

3 In a separate bowl, beat butter and sugar at high speed until light and fluffy.

4 Reduce speed and mix in egg, egg white and vanilla extract.

5 Add flour mixture to butter mixture in 3 batches, alternating with buttermilk, and mixing on low speed after each addition. Beat at high speed for 1 minute until thoroughly combined. Fold in 3 tablespoons of caramel.

6 Pour batter into cupcake liners and cake pan until ⅔ full. Bake cupcakes for about 15 minutes and the cake for about 25 minutes or until a toothpick inserted in the center comes out clean. Set aside to cool.

7 Frost the cupcakes and cake, and then drizzle with remaining homemade caramel. Serve immediately or refrigerate for up to 2 days in an airtight container.

Bring on the Brownies Cupcake Cake

This melt-in-your mouth masterpiece is perfect for youngsters who love chocolate! If your celebrating a birthday, just arrange the cupcakes in the shape of the birthday boy or girl's age!

Makes 25 small cupcakes

Ingredients

Cupcakes

2 ounces dark chocolate, chopped
4 ounces unsalted butter, room
　　temperature
2 large eggs
1 cup sugar
⅓ cup all-purpose flour

Frosting

2 cups confectioners' sugar
¼ cup water
1 teaspoon vanilla extract
Food coloring, optional

Garnish

Chocolate candies

Cupcakes

1 Preheat oven to 350°F and line a cupcake pan with paper liners.

2 Place chocolate and butter in the top of a double boiler and heat over medium-high heat until melted. Mix together until smooth.

3 Remove mixture from heat and transfer to a medium bowl. Stir eggs, sugar and flour until thoroughly blended.

4 Pour batter into cupcake liners until ⅔ full and bake for about 15 minutes or until a toothpick, inserted in the center of a cupcake, comes out clean. Set aside to cool.

Frosting

5 Place confectioners' sugar, water and vanilla extract in a bowl. Mix thoroughly until smooth. Tint with food coloring.

6 Drizzle icing over the brownie cupcakes and sprinkle with chocolate candies. Serve immediately or refrigerate for up to 2 days in an airtight container.

Caterpillar Cutie Cupcake Cake

Delight a party of toddlers with this adorable caterpillar cake. Use favorite candies to make the feet and face, and have extras on hand for nibbling.

Makes 15 regular cupcakes and one 6-inch round cake

Ingredients

Cupcakes

3 cups cake flour

3 teaspoons baking powder

Pinch salt

6½ ounces unsalted butter, room
   temperature

2 cups sugar

2 large eggs

2 large egg whites

2 teaspoons vanilla extract

1 cup buttermilk

1 cup chocolate chips

2 batches Vanilla Frosting (page 16)

Green food coloring

Garnish

Black gummy candies

Green sprinkles

Red licorice

Plastic eyes

Red pipe cleaner

1 Preheat oven to 350°F. Line a cupcake pan with paper liners and generously grease a 6-inch round cake pan.

2 In a medium bowl, sift together flour, baking powder and salt.

3 In a separate bowl, beat butter and sugar at high speed until light and fluffy.

4 Reduce speed and mix in eggs, egg whites and vanilla extract.

5 Add flour mixture to butter mixture in 3 batches, alternating with buttermilk, and mixing on low speed after each addition. Beat at high speed for 1 minute until thoroughly combined. Fold in the chocolate chips.

6 Pour batter into cupcake liners and cake pan until ⅔ full. Bake the cupcakes for about 10 minutes and the cake for about 25 minutes, or until a toothpick inserted in the center comes out clean. Set aside to cool.

7 Tint the frosting with green food coloring and then frost the cupcakes and cake. Decorate cupcakes with green sprinkles and create a candy face on the cake using licorice, gummy candies, plastic eyes and pipe cleaners.

8 Serve immediately or refrigerate for up to 2 days in an airtight container.

Double Trouble Cupcake Cake

These cupcakes have double the chocolate and double the fun. Stack them in tiny towers, so that everyone gets a double serving!

Makes 10 regular cupcakes
and 10 small cupcakes

Ingredients

Cupcakes

1¼ cups cake flour

¼ cup cocoa powder

1½ teaspoons baking powder

Pinch salt

3¼ ounces unsalted butter, room
   temperature

1 cup demerara sugar

1 large egg

1 large egg white

1 teaspoon vanilla extract

½ cup buttermilk

Frosting

2 ounces dark chocolate, chopped

3½ ounces unsalted butter, room
   temperature

2½ cups confectioners' sugar

3 tablespoons milk

Garnish

Rainbow sprinkles

Cupcakes

1 Preheat oven to 350°F and line a cupcake pan with paper liners.

2 In a medium bowl, mix together flour, cocoa, baking powder and salt.

3 In a separate bowl, beat butter and sugar at high speed until light and fluffy.

4 Reduce speed, mix in egg, egg white and vanilla extract.

5 Add flour mixture to butter mixture in 3 batches, alternating with buttermilk, and mixing on low speed after each addition. Beat at high speed for 1 minute until thoroughly combined.

6 Pour batter into cupcake liners until ⅔ full. Bake for about 15 minutes, until a toothpick inserted in the center comes out clean. Small cupcakes will be ready first. Set aside to cool.

Frosting

7 Melt chocolate in the top of a double boiler, and then set aside to cool until warm to the touch.

8 In the bowl of an electric mixer, beat butter, confectioners' sugar and milk at high speed until light and fluffy. Fold in the melted chocolate.

9 Frost the cupcakes and decorate with rainbow sprinkles. Serve immediately or refrigerate for up to 2 days in an airtight container.

Ice Cream Parlor Cupcake Cake

Disguise a batch or two of cupcakes by dressing them up in ice cream cones! This cake is a perfect chance to indulge in over-the-top frostings, so pull out the pastel food coloring!

Makes 24 small cupcakes

Ingredients

Cupcakes

1½ cups cake flour

1½ teaspoons baking powder

Pinch salt

3¼ ounces unsalted butter, room temperature

1 cup sugar

1 large egg

1 large egg white

1 teaspoon vanilla extract

½ cup buttermilk

⅓ cup small white chocolate chips

2 batches Vanilla Frosting (page 16)

Green food coloring

Orange food coloring

Pink food coloring

Garnish

Fresh cherries

Chocolate sprinkles

Cinnamon heart candies

Rainbow sprinkles

Cupcake Cake Idea

• • • • • • • • • • • • • • • •

- **24 ice cream cones**
- **24-cupcake tree stand**

Insert each cupcake into an ice cream cone and insert each ice cream cone into one of the holders on the tree stand.

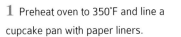

1 Preheat oven to 350°F and line a cupcake pan with paper liners.

2 In a medium bowl, sift together flour, baking powder and salt.

3 In a separate bowl, beat butter and sugar at high speed until light and fluffy.

4 Reduce speed and mix in egg, egg white and vanilla extract.

5 Add flour mixture to butter mixture in 3 batches, alternating with buttermilk, and mixing on low speed after each addition. Beat at high speed for 1 minute until thoroughly combined. Fold in the white chocolate chips.

6 Pour batter into cupcake liners until ⅔ full. Bake for about 15 minutes or until a toothpick inserted in the center comes out clean. Set aside to cool.

7 Divide frosting evenly into four small bowls. Leave one bowl of frosting white and tint the other bowls of frosting green, orange and pink respectively.

8 Frost each cupcake with one color of frosting and place a star of white frosting on top. Decorate with cherries, sprinkles and candy hearts. Serve immediately or refrigerate for up to 2 days in an airtight container.

Magic Marshmallow Mountain Cupcake Cake

Even if it's not the season for lighting a bonfire, you can still enjoy melted mini marshmallows. Have plenty of extra marshmallows on hand for hungry guests.

Cupcake Cake Idea

- Toothpicks*
- Cake stand

Insert a toothpick partway into the bottom of each cupcake and affix the cupcakes around the edge of cake. Place the cake on the cake stand and scatter marshmallows all around.

* Remove toothpicks before serving.

Makes 5 small cupcakes
and one 6-inch round cake

Ingredients

Cupcakes

1 cup cake flour

1½ teaspoons baking powder

Pinch salt

1½ ounces unsalted butter, room
    temperature

¾ cup sugar

1 large egg

1 large egg white

1 teaspoon vanilla extract

½ cup buttermilk

¾ cup mini marshmallows

Basic Chocolate Frosting (page 16)

Garnish

Gummy candies

1 Preheat oven to 350°F. Line a cupcake pan with paper liners and generously grease a 6-inch round cake pan.

2 In a medium bowl, sift together flour, baking powder and salt.

3 In a separate bowl, beat butter and sugar at high speed until light and fluffy.

4 Reduce speed and mix in egg, egg white and vanilla extract.

5 Add flour mixture to butter mixture in 3 batches, alternating with buttermilk, and mixing on low speed after each addition. Beat at high speed for 1 minute until thoroughly combined. Fold in the mini marshmallows.

6 Pour batter into cupcake liners and cake pan until ⅔ full. Bake the cupcakes for about 15 minutes and the cake for about 25 minutes until a toothpick inserted in the center comes out clean. Set aside to cool.

7 Frost the cupcakes and cake and decorate with gummy candies. Serve immediately or refrigerate for up to 2 days in an airtight container.

Luck 'o' the Irish Cupcake Cake

(photo page 7)

The lovely texture and flavor of creamy Irish whisky makes it perfect for integrating into adult desserts. Serve with steaming hot Irish coffee.

Cupcake Cake Idea

· Luck 'o' the Irish Cupcake Cake
· Salted Chocolate Cupcake Cake (page 44)
· 4-tier cupcake stand

Place the mini cupcakes around the edges of each tier on the cake stand and the regular cupcakes on the inside.

Makes 36 mini cupcakes

Ingredients

Cupcakes

1½ cups cake flour

1½ teaspoons baking powder

Pinch salt

3¼ ounces unsalted butter, room temperature

1 cup sugar

1 large egg

1 large egg white

1 teaspoon vanilla extract

½ cup buttermilk

Frosting

3¼ ounces unsalted butter, room temperature

3 cups confectioners' sugar

2 tablespoons Irish cream whisky (such as Bailey's Irish Cream)

Garnish

Crushed chocolate

Cupcakes

1 Preheat oven to 350°F and line a cupcake pan with paper liners. In a medium bowl, sift together flour, baking powder and salt. In a separate bowl, beat butter and sugar at high speed until light and fluffy. Reduce speed and mix in egg, egg white and vanilla extract.

2 Add flour mixture to butter mixture in 3 batches, alternating with buttermilk, and mixing on low speed after each addition. Beat at high speed for 1 minute until thoroughly combined.

3 Pour batter into cupcake liners until ⅔ full. Bake for about 15 minutes or until a toothpick inserted in the center comes out clean. Set aside to cool.

Frosting

4 In the bowl of an electric mixer, beat butter, confectioners' sugar and whisky at high speed for about 4 minutes, until light and fluffy. Frost the cupcakes and sprinkle with crushed chocolate wafers. Serve immediately or refrigerate for up to 2 days in an airtight container.

Lovely Lavender Cupcake Cake

The delicate flavor of lavender sugar makes these cakes perfect for serving at teatime. To make lavender sugar, place white sugar and dried lavender flowers in an airtight glass jar for a couple of weeks.

Makes 9 regular cupcakes, 12 small cupcakes and one 7-inch round cake

Ingredients

Cupcakes

3 cups cake flour

3 teaspoons baking powder

Pinch salt

6½ ounces unsalted butter, room
    temperature

2 cups lavender sugar

2 large eggs

2 large egg whites

2 teaspoons vanilla extract

1 cup buttermilk

2 batches Vanilla Frosting (page 16)

Light purple food coloring

Garnish

Lavender petals

Cupcake Cake Idea

- Toothpicks*
- One 8-inch round plate
- 9 teacups

Insert a toothpick in the middle top of each regular cupcake and affix a small cupcake on top. Insert a toothpick into the bottom of the remaining small cupcakes and affix on the center of the cake. Place the cake on a cake plate and each 2-tier cupcake in a teacup.

* Remove toothpicks before serving.

1 Preheat oven to 350°F. Line the small cupcake pan with metallic liners and the regular cupcake pan with paper liners. Generously grease a 7-inch round cake pan.

2 In a medium bowl, sift together flour, baking powder and salt.

3 In a separate bowl, beat butter and lavender sugar at high speed until light and fluffy.

4 Reduce speed and mix in eggs, egg whites and vanilla extract.

5 Add flour mixture to butter mixture in 3 batches, alternating with buttermilk, and mixing on low speed after each addition. Beat at high speed for 1 minute until thoroughly combined.

6 Pour batter into cupcake liners and cake pan until ⅔ full. Bake the cupcakes for about 15 minutes and the cake for about 30 minutes, or until a toothpick inserted in the center comes out clean. Set aside to cool.

7 Set aside about ⅓ of the frosting for tinting later, and use the rest to frost the regular cupcakes and cake. Sprinkle dried lavender petals all around the cake.

8 Tint the remaining frosting with light purple food coloring, and then frost the small cupcakes. Top each small cupcake with a few dried lavender flowers. Serve immediately or refrigerate for up to 2 days in an airtight container.

Salted Chocolate Cupcake Cake

(photo page 7)

Planning a party for people with sophisticated palates?
Here's a recipe that's sure to impress. For the best flavor,
use dark chocolate with at least 70% cocoa solids content
for the frosting.

Cupcake Cake Idea

• **Luck 'o' the Irish Cupcake Cake** (page 39)
• **Salted Chocolate Cupcake Cake**
• **4-tier cupcake stand**

Place the mini cupcakes around the edges of each tier on the cake stand and the regular cupcakes on the inside.

Makes 12 regular cupcakes

Ingredients

Cupcakes

1⅓ cups cake flour
½ cup cocoa powder
1½ teaspoons baking powder
Pinch salt
3¼ ounces unsalted butter, room
   temperature
1 cup sugar
1 large egg
1 large egg white
1 teaspoon vanilla extract
½ cup buttermilk

Frosting

1½ ounces dark chocolate, chopped
1 tablespoon salt
3 ounces unsalted butter, room
   temperature
2½ cups confectioners' sugar
3 tablespoons milk

Garnish

1 tablespoon coarse sea salt

Cupcakes

1 Preheat oven to 350°F and line a cupcake pan with paper liners. In a medium bowl, sift together flour, cocoa, baking powder and salt. In a separate bowl, beat butter and sugar at high speed until light and fluffy. Reduce speed and mix in egg, egg white and vanilla.

2 Add flour mixture to butter mixture in 3 batches, alternating with buttermilk, and mixing on low speed after each addition. Beat at high speed for 1 minute until thoroughly combined. Pour batter into cupcake pan until ⅔ full and bake for 15 minutes or until a toothpick inserted in the center comes out clean. Set aside to cool.

Frosting

3 Place chocolate and salt in the top of a double boiler, and heat over medium-high heat until melted. Set aside to cool until warm to the touch. In the bowl of an electric mixer, beat butter, confectioners' sugar and milk at high speed until light and fluffy. Fold in the salted chocolate. Frost the cupcakes and sprinkle with a bit of sea salt. Serve immediately or transfer to an airtight container and refrigerate for up to 2 days.

Heavenly Halva Cupcake Cake

Here's something to satisfy the sophisticated sweet tooth: chocolate cupcakes topped with nutty tahini frosting and sweet floss halva. An intriguing combination.

Makes 16 mini cupcakes and one 4-inch round cake

Ingredients

Cupcakes

1⅓ cups cake flour

½ cup cocoa powder

1½ teaspoons baking powder

Pinch salt

3¼ ounces unsalted butter, room temperature

1 cup demerara sugar

1 large egg

1 large egg white

1 teaspoon vanilla extract

½ cup buttermilk

Frosting

3¼ ounces unsalted butter, room temperature

2½ cups confectioners' sugar

2 tablespoons milk

2 tablespoons tahini

Garnish

Floss halva

Cupcake Cake Idea

· **2-tier cake stand**

Arrange the cupcakes on the bottom tier of a 2-tier cake stand and place the cake on the top tier.

Cupcakes

1 Preheat oven to 350°F. Line a cupcake pan with paper liners and generously grease a 4-inch round cake pan. In a medium bowl, sift together flour, cocoa, baking powder and salt. In a separate bowl, beat butter and sugar at high speed until light and fluffy. Reduce speed and mix in egg, egg white and vanilla extract.

2 Add flour mixture to butter mixture in 3 batches, alternating with buttermilk, and mixing on low speed after each addition. Beat at high speed for 1 minute until thoroughly combined.

3 Pour batter into the cupcake liners and cake pan until ⅔ full. Bake the cupcakes for about 15 minutes and the cake for about 25 minutes or until a toothpick inserted in the center comes out clean. Set aside to cool.

Frosting

4 In the bowl of an electric mixer, beat butter, confectioners' sugar, milk and tahini at high speed until light and fluffy. Frost the cupcakes and cake and decorate with floss halva. Serve immediately.

Royally Rum Raisin Cupcake Cake

Even if you're not expecting the Queen at your party, there's no reason you shouldn't be prepared to host a princess or two. For best flavor, soak the raisins overnight in the rum.

~~~~~~

Makes 12 regular cupcakes

Ingredients

Cupcakes

⅓ cup raisins

⅓ cup rum

1⅓ cups cake flour

½ cup cocoa powder

1½ teaspoons baking powder

Pinch salt

3¼ ounces unsalted butter, room temperature

1 cup demerara sugar

1 large egg

1 large egg white

½ cup buttermilk

Frosting

1 cup heavy whipping cream, cold

3 teaspoons sugar

1 teaspoon vanilla extract

2 tablespoons rum

Garnish

Chocolate curls

Cupcake Cake Idea

· **Traditional tea tray**
· **Tea pot**

Place the tea pot in the middle of the tea tray and arrange the cupcakes all around.

Cupcakes

1 Place raisins in a small bowl. Pour in rum to cover raisins and soak for 24 hours. Preheat oven to 350°F. Line a cupcake pan with paper liners. In a medium bowl, sift together flour, cocoa, baking powder and salt. In a separate bowl, beat butter and sugar at high speed until light and fluffy. Reduce speed and mix in egg and egg white.

2 Add flour mixture to butter mixture in 3 batches, alternating with buttermilk, and mixing on low speed after each addition. Beat at high speed for 1 minute until thoroughly combined. Fold in the rum-soaked raisins.

3 Pour batter into cupcake liners until ⅔ full and bake for about 15 minutes, or until a toothpick inserted in the center comes out clean. Set aside to cool.

Frosting

4 Place cream in bowl and whip. When it starts to thicken, add sugar, vanilla and rum. Continue whipping until stiff peaks form. Frost the cupcakes and garnish with chocolate curls. Serve immediately or refrigerate for up to 2 days in an airtight container.

Daringly Date Cupcake Cake

This cake is just right for bringing to an office birthday party, since it's perfect for serving at mid-morning coffee breaks. If your coworkers are fond of sweets, you might want to make a double batch.

Makes 24 small cupcakes

Ingredients

Cupcakes

7 ounces pitted dates, chopped

1 teaspoon vanilla extract

¾ teaspoon baking soda

6 ounces boiling water

1⅔ cups cake flour

2 teaspoons baking powder

¼ teaspoon salt

3¼ ounces unsalted butter, room
   temperature

1 cup light brown sugar

2 large eggs

Vanilla Frosting (page16)

1 Preheat oven to 350°F and line a cupcake pan with paper liners.

2 In a heatproof bowl or small pot, combine dates, vanilla extract and baking soda. Pour in boiling water to cover, and then set aside to cool.

3 In another bowl, sift together flour, baking power and salt.

4 In a medium bowl, beat butter and sugar for 2 minutes until light and fluffy. Beat in eggs until combined.

5 Mix in flour mixture until combined. Then fold in the date mixture.

6 Pour batter in cupcake liners until ⅔ full. Bake for about 20 minutes or until a toothpick inserted in the center comes out clean. Set aside to cool.

7 Frost the cupcakes with vanilla frosting. Serve immediately or refrigerate for up to 2 days in an airtight container.

Triple Chocolate Cupcake Cake

Here's a great gift for a dear chocophile: an indulgent cake with chocolate liqueur, chocolate ganâche and chocolate curls. Serve with fresh espresso or cappuccino.

Cupcake Cake Idea

· **Toothpicks***

Make ten 2-tiered cupcake cakes by inserting a toothpick in the middle top of a regular cupcake and the middle of the bottom of a small cupcake.

*** Remove toothpicks before serving.**

Makes 10 regular cupcakes and 10 small cupcakes

Ingredients

Cupcakes

1¼ cups cake flour

½ cup cocoa powder

1½ teaspoons baking powder

Pinch salt

3¼ ounces unsalted butter, room
   temperature

¾ cup sugar

1 large egg

1 large egg white

1 teaspoon vanilla extract

½ cup buttermilk

Ganâche

8 ounces dark chocolate, chopped

¼ cup heavy cream

¼ cup chocolate liqueur

Garnish

Chocolate curls

Cupcakes

1 Preheat oven to 350°F and line a cupcake pan with paper liners. In a medium bowl, sift together flour, cocoa, baking powder and salt. In a separate bowl, beat butter and sugar at high speed until light and fluffy. Reduce speed and mix in egg, egg white and vanilla extract.

2 Add flour mixture to butter mixture in 3 batches, alternating with buttermilk, and mixing on low speed after each addition. Beat at high speed for 1 minute until thoroughly combined.

3 Pour batter into cupcake liners until ⅔ full. Bake for about 15 minutes, or until a toothpick inserted in the center comes out clean. Set aside to cool.

Ganâche

4 Place chocolate in the top of a double boiler and melt over low heat. Remove from heat and stir in cream and liqueur. Remove the center of each cupcake using a sharp knife (Be sure to leave a bit of cupcake base at the bottom.) Spoon some ganâche into the hole and drizzle on top. Sprinkle with chocolate curls. Serve immediately or refrigerate for up to 2 days in an airtight container.

Minty Masterpiece Cupcake Cake

Celebrating a grown-up birthday doesn't mean you can't have some fun. These gorgeous cupcakes feature fun polka dot frosting and sprigs of fresh mint. Serve with mint tea.

**Makes 6 small cupcakes
and one 4-inch round cake**

Ingredients

Cupcakes

1⅓ cups cake flour

½ cup cocoa powder

1½ teaspoons baking powder

Pinch salt

3¼ ounces unsalted butter, room
  temperature

1 cup demerara sugar

1 large egg

1 large egg white

1 teaspoon vanilla extract

½ cup buttermilk

Frosting

3¼ ounces unsalted butter, room
  temperature

2½ cups confectioners' sugar

1 tablespoon milk

Green food coloring, optional

1 teaspoon peppermint extract

3 tablespoons dark chocolate chips

Garnish

Fresh mint sprigs

Cupcake Cake Idea

· **Cake stand**

Place the cake at the center of the cake stand and arrange the cupcakes all around.

Cupcakes

1 Preheat oven to 350°F. Line a cupcake pan with paper liners and generously grease a 4-inch round cake pan. In a medium bowl, sift together flour, cocoa, baking powder and salt.
In a separate bowl, beat butter and sugar at high speed until light and fluffy. Reduce speed and mix in egg, egg white and vanilla extract.

2 Add flour mixture to butter mixture in 3 batches, alternating with buttermilk, and mixing on low speed after each addition. Beat at high speed for 1 minute until thoroughly combined.

3 Pour batter into cupcake liner and cake pan until ⅔ full. Bake the cupcakes for about 10 minutes and the cake for about 25 minutes, or until a toothpick inserted in the center comes out clean. Set aside to cool.

Frosting

4 In the bowl of an electric mixer, beat butter, confectioners' sugar, milk, food coloring and peppermint extract at high speed until light and fluffy. Fold in the chocolate chips. Don't overfold, so that the chocolate doesn't melt or discolor the frosting. Frost the cupcakes and the cake, and then garnish each cupcake with fresh mint. Serve immediately or refrigerate for up to 2 days in an airtight container.

Berry Beautiful Cupcake Cake and Sweet Strawberry Cupcake Cake (page 53)

Berry Beautiful Cupcake Cake

Preparing a party for someone who's pretty in pink? Pamper her with this gorgeous cake collection. For a really pretty presentation, tint the frosting to match your accessories.

Makes 24 mini cupcakes

Ingredients

Cupcakes

1½ cups cake flour

1½ teaspoons baking powder

Pinch salt

3¼ ounces unsalted butter, room temperature

1 cup sugar

1 large egg

1 large egg white

1 teaspoon lemon extract

3 tablespoons lemon zest

½ cup buttermilk

Frosting

3 ounces unsalted butter, room temperature

3 cups confectioners' sugar

1 tablespoon milk

2 tablespoons raspberry jam, with high fruit content

Cupcake Cake Idea
● ● ● ● ● ● ● ● ● ● ● ● ● ● ●

· **Berry Beautiful
Cupcake Cake**
· **Sweet Strawberry
Cupcake Cake** (page 53)
· **Pink 3-tier cupcake stand**
· **Pink accessories and candies**

Arrange the cupcakes on the cake stand
and decorate the table with matching
accessories and candies.

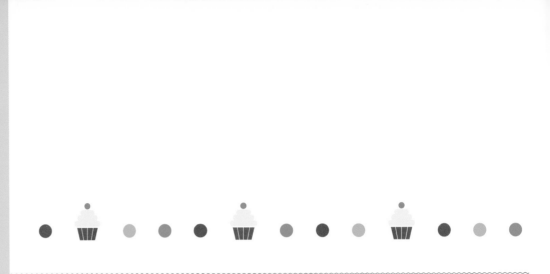

Cupcakes

1 Preheat oven to 350°F and line a
cupcake pan with metallic liners.

2 In a medium bowl, sift together flour,
baking powder and salt.

3 In a separate bowl, beat butter and
sugar at high speed until light and fluffy.
Reduce speed and mix in egg, egg
white, lemon extract and lemon zest.

4 Add flour mixture to butter mixture in
3 batches, alternating with buttermilk,
and mixing on low speed after each
addition. Beat at high speed for about
1 minute until thoroughly combined.

5 Pour batter into cupcake liners until
⅔ full and bake cupcakes for 20 minutes
or until a toothpick inserted in the center
comes out clean. Set aside to cool.

Frosting

6 In the bowl of an electric mixer, beat
butter, confectioners' sugar and milk
until light and fluffy. Mix in the jam until
smooth.

7 Frost the cupcakes and serve
immediately or refrigerate for up to
2 days in an airtight container.

Sweet Strawberry Cupcake Cake

You don't need fresh strawberries to make these delightful cupcakes; just a bit of strawberry jam. In addition to sweetening the frosting, the jam gives it a lovely light pink color.

Makes 12 regular cupcakes

Ingredients

Cupcakes

1½ cups cake flour

1½ teaspoons baking powder

Pinch salt

3¼ ounces unsalted butter, room temperature

1 cup sugar

1 large egg

1 large egg white

1 teaspoon vanilla extract

½ cup buttermilk

½ cup white chocolate chips

Jam Frosting (page 17)

Garnish

Red heart candy confetti

Cupcake Cake Idea

· Berry Beautiful Cupcake Cake (page 51)
· Sweet Strawberry Cupcake Cake
· Pink 3-tier cupcake stand
· Pink accessories and candies

Arrange the cupcakes on the cake stand and decorate the table with matching accessories and candies.

1 Preheat oven to 350°F and line a cupcake pan with paper liners. In a medium bowl, sift together flour, baking powder and salt. In a separate bowl, beat butter and sugar at high speed until light and fluffy. Reduce speed and mix in egg, egg white and vanilla extract.

2 Add flour mixture to butter mixture in three batches, alternating with buttermilk, and mixing on low speed after each addition. Beat at high speed for about 1 minute until thoroughly combined. Fold in the chocolate chips.

3 Pour batter into cupcake liners until ⅔ full and bake for about 20 minutes, or until a toothpick inserted in the center comes out clean. Set aside to cool.

4 Frost the cupcakes and garnish with red heart confetti. Serve immediately or refrigerate for up to 2 days in an airtight container.

Fancy Floral Cupcake Cake

Who would have thought flowers could be so tasty! These flower cakes feature rich chocolatey cupcakes and creamy bright frosting. Arranged on pretty doilies, they make a lovely centerpiece.

Makes 21 regular cupcakes

Ingredients

Cupcakes

2⅔ cups cake flour

½ cup cocoa powder

3 teaspoons baking powder

Pinch salt

6½ ounces unsalted butter, room
    temperature

2 cups demerara sugar

2 large eggs

2 large egg whites

2 teaspoons vanilla extract

1 cup buttermilk

Frosting

6 ounces unsalted butter, room
    temperature

5 cups confectioners' sugar

2 tablespoons milk

2 teaspoons vanilla extract

Brown food coloring

Pink food coloring

Garnish

Black gummy candies

Cupcakes

1 Preheat oven to 350°F and line a cupcake pan with paper liners.

2 In a medium bowl, sift together flour, cocoa, baking powder and salt.

3 In a separate bowl, beat butter and sugar at high speed until light and fluffy.

4 Reduce speed and mix in eggs, egg whites and vanilla extract.

5 Add flour mixture to butter mixture in 3 batches, alternating with buttermilk, and mixing on low speed after each addition.

6 Beat at high speed for 1 minute until thoroughly combined.

7 Pour batter into cupcake liners until ⅔ full and bake for about 20 minutes, or until a toothpick inserted in the center comes out clean. Set aside to cool.

Frosting

8 In the bowl of an electric mixer, beat butter, confectioners' sugar, milk and vanilla extract at high speed until light and fluffy.

9 Place ⅙ of the frosting in a small bowl and tint with brown food coloring. Tint the rest of the frosting with pink food coloring.

10 Frost 3 cupcakes with brown frosting and top with gummy candies. Frost the rest of the cupcakes with pink frosting. Serve immediately or refrigerate for up to 2 days in an airtight container.

It's a Girl! Cupcake Cake

Peppermint and chocolate are natural playmates, and they're perfectly suited in this pretty display. Tint the frostings until you achieve just the right shade of pink and accessorize with matching candies.

Makes 24 small cupcakes

Ingredients

Cupcakes

1½ cups cake flour

1½ teaspoons baking powder

Pinch salt

3¼ ounces unsalted butter, room temperature

1 cup sugar

1 large egg

1 large egg white

1 teaspoon vanilla extract

½ cup buttermilk

Basic Chocolate Frosting (page 16)

Peppermint Frosting (page 17)

Light pink food coloring

Dark pink food coloring

Garnish

Baby-themed sugar decorations

Cupcakes

1 Preheat oven to 350°F and line a cupcake pan with paper liners. In a medium bowl, sift together flour, baking powder and salt.

2 In a separate bowl, beat butter and sugar at high speed until light and fluffy. Reduce speed and mix in egg, egg white and vanilla extract.

3 Add flour mixture to butter mixture in 3 batches, alternating with buttermilk, and mixing on low speed after each addition. Beat at high speed for 1 minute until thoroughly combined.

4 Pour batter into cupcake liners until ⅔ full and bake for about 20 minutes, or until a toothpick inserted in the center comes out clean. Set aside to cool.

5 Pipe chocolate frosting in a ring around the top of each cupcake. Tint ⅔ of the peppermint frosting with light pink frosting and frost the top of each cupcake, inside the ring of chocolate.

6 Tint the remaining ⅓ of the peppermint frosting with dark pink food coloring and pipe letters onto the cupcakes to spell your message.

7 Decorate the cupcakes that don't have letters with sugar decorations. Serve immediately or refrigerate for up to 2 days in an airtight container.

Momma Knows Best Zesty Cupcake Cake

Light and zesty, this dessert is perfect for serving at an afternoon affair. Serve cake slices first and let guests who want seconds help themselves to a cupcake or two.

Cupcake Cake Idea

· **Toothpicks***

Insert a toothpick halfway into the bottom of each cupcake and affix the cupcakes in a floral shape on the middle of the cake.

* **Remove toothpicks before serving.**

Makes 5 small cupcakes and one 8-inch round cake

Ingredients

Cupcakes

2½ cups self-rising flour

Pinch salt

3 large eggs

1 cup sugar

3 teaspoons finely grated orange zest

3 teaspoons finely grated lemon zest

¾ cup olive oil

⅓ cup milk

⅓ cup orange juice

Royal Icing (page 18)

Garnish

½ cup candied lemon peel

1 Preheat oven to 350°F. Line a cupcake pan with paper liners and generously grease an 8-inch cake pan.

2 In a medium bowl, sift together flour and salt.

3 In another bowl, place eggs and sugar, and mix until light and fluffy.

4 Reduce speed. Add orange zest and lemon zest, and mix. Stir in olive oil.

5 Add flour mixture to butter mixture in 3 batches, alternating with milk and orange juice, and mixing on low speed after each addition. Beat at high speed for 1 minute until thoroughly combined.

6 Pour batter into cupcake liners and cake pan until ⅔ full. Bake the cupcakes for about 15 minutes and the cake for about 25 minutes, or until a toothpick inserted in the center comes out clean. Set aside to cool.

7 Drizzle icing on the cake and cupcakes, and then garnish with candied lemon peel. Serve immediately or refrigerate for up to 2 days in an airtight container.

Bouncing Baby Cupcake Cake

These cream cheese cupcakes are easy to make, so they're just right for serving at an affair when you have your hands full with other things…like bouncing new babies!

Makes 12 regular cupcakes

Ingredients

Cupcakes

1⅓ cups cake flour

¼ cup cocoa powder

¾ teaspoon baking soda

¾ cup + ¼ cup sugar

¼ cup sunflower oil

¾ cup water

2 teaspoons white vinegar

1 teaspoon vanilla extract

5½ ounces cream cheese

1 large egg

½ cup chocolate chips

1 Preheat oven to 350°F and line a cupcake pan with paper liners.

2 In a medium bowl, sift together flour, cocoa and baking soda. Mix in ¾ cup sugar.

3 Add oil, water, vinegar and vanilla extract. Mix until completely combined.

4 In a separate bowl, combine remaining ¼ cup sugar with the cream cheese and egg. Fold in the chocolate chips.

5 Pour flour mixture into cupcake liners, filling them ⅔ full. Place a spoon of the cream cheese mixture on the top of each cupcake. Bake for about 25 minutes or until firm.

6 Transfer to a wire rack to cool, then chill until ready to serve. May be refrigerated in an airtight container for up to 2 days.

It's a Boy! Cupcake Cake

White cupcakes are easily adaptable for any occasion. To prepare this cake for a party celebrating a new baby boy, bake them in blue paper liners and decorate your party with matching accessories.

Makes 18 regular cupcakes and one 4-inch square cake

Ingredients

Cupcakes

2½ cups all-purpose flour

3 teaspoons baking powder

½ cup shredded sweetened coconut

½ teaspoon salt

6½ ounces unsalted butter, room temperature

2 cups sugar

2 large eggs

2 large egg whites

2 teaspoons vanilla extract

1 cup coconut milk

Frosting

6½ ounces unsalted butter, room temperature

5 cups confectioners' sugar

2 tablespoons coconut milk

2 teaspoons coconut extract

Garnish

1½ cups shredded sweetened coconut

2 tablespoons tiny silver decoration balls

- **3-tier cake stand**
- **Blue and white accessories**

Place the cake on the top tier of the cake stand and arrange the cupcakes on the bottom tiers. Decorate the table with blue and white accessories.

Cupcakes

1 Preheat oven to 350°F. Line a cupcake pan with blue and white paper liners and generously grease a 4-inch square cake pan.

2 In a medium bowl, sift together flour, baking powder, coconut and salt.

3 In a separate bowl, beat butter and sugar at high speed until light and fluffy.

4 Reduce speed and mix in eggs, egg whites and vanilla extract.

5 Add flour mixture to butter mixture in 3 batches, alternating with coconut milk, and mixing on low speed after each addition. Beat at high speed for 1 minute until thoroughly combined.

6 Pour batter into cupcake liners and cake pan until ⅔ full. Bake the cupcakes for about 15 minutes and the cake for about 25 minutes, or until a toothpick inserted in the center comes out clean. Set aside to cool.

Frosting

7 In the bowl of an electric mixer, beat butter, confectioners' sugar, coconut milk and coconut extract at high speed until light and fluffy.

8 Frost the cupcakes and cake and then garnish the cupcakes with shredded coconut and the cake with silver decoration balls. Serve immediately or refrigerate for up to 2 days in an airtight container.

I Do...I Really Do Cupcake Cake

This elegant design features easy yet elegant frosting techniques. Just pipe a dollop of frosting onto each cupcake and frost the cake using an offset spatula.

Makes 45 small cupcakes and one 6-inch round cake

Ingredients

Cupcakes

7½ cups cake flour

7½ teaspoons baking powder

Pinch salt

16¼ ounces unsalted butter, room temperature

5 cups sugar

5 large eggs

5 large egg whites

5 teaspoons vanilla extract

2½ cups buttermilk

Frosting

15 ounces unsalted butter, room temperature

12½ cups confectioners' sugar

5 tablespoons milk

4 tablespoons pomegranate syrup

Cupcake Cake Idea

- **3-tier cake stand**
- **Fresh flowers**

Place a single flower on each cupcake and several flowers on the cake. Place the cake on the top tier of the cake stand and place the cupcakes on the middle and bottom tier.

Cupcakes

1 Preheat oven to 350°F. Line cupcake pans with paper liners and generously grease a 6-inch round cake pan.

2 In a medium bowl, mix together flour, baking powder and salt.

3 In another bowl, beat the butter and sugar at a high speed with an electric whisk until light and fluffy.

4 Reduce the speed and mix in the eggs, egg whites and vanilla extract.

5 Add flour mixture to butter mixture in 3 batches, alternating with buttermilk, and mixing on low speed after each addition. Beat at high speed for 1 minute until thoroughly combined.

6 Pour batter into cupcake liners and cake pan until ⅔ full. Bake the cupcakes for about 18 minutes and the cake for about 25 minutes, or until a toothpick inserted in the center comes out clean. Set aside to cool.

Frosting

7 In the bowl of an electric mixer, beat butter, confectioners' sugar and milk at high speed until light and fluffy. Mix in the pomegranate syrup, 1 tablespoon at a time, until evenly combined.

8 Frost the cupcakes and cake and serve immediately, or refrigerate for up to 2 days in an airtight container.

Cherish the Love Cupcake Cake

*Chocolate is a natural for serving at weddings.
Add silver balls for decoration and integrate a few chocolate
hearts and you've created an elegant, melt-in-your mouth treat!*

Cupcake Cake Idea

· 3-tier silver cupcake stand
· Silver foil-covered chocolate hearts

Arrange the cupcakes and chocolate hearts on each tier of the cupcake stand.

Makes 12 regular cupcakes

Ingredients

Cupcakes

1¼ cups cake flour

¼ cup cocoa powder

1½ teaspoons baking powder

Pinch salt

3¼ ounces unsalted butter, room
   temperature

1 cup brown sugar

1 large egg

1 large egg white

1 teaspoon vanilla extract

½ cup buttermilk

Chocolate Ganâche (page 18)

Garnish

Silver balls

1 Preheat oven to 350°F and line a cupcake pan with paper liners.

2 In a medium bowl, mix together flour, cocoa, baking powder and salt. In a separate bowl, beat butter and sugar at high speed until light and fluffy.

3 Reduce speed, mix in egg, egg white and vanilla extract.

4 Add flour mixture to butter mixture in 3 batches, alternating with buttermilk, and mixing on low speed after each addition. Beat at high speed for 1 minute until thoroughly combined.

5 Pour batter into cupcake liners until ⅔ full and bake for about 15 minutes, or until a toothpick inserted in the center comes out clean. Set aside to cool.

6 Frost each cupcake with chocolate ganâche and decorate with silver balls. Serve immediately or refrigerate for up to 2 days in an airtight container.

Be My Honey Cupcake Cake

Almonds, associated with health and prosperity, are often served as wedding favors. In this delightful cake, they are teamed deliciously with honey for sweet luck!

Cupcake Cake Idea

- **24-cupcake tree stand**
- **Bags of sugared almonds**

Insert each cupcake into a holder in the tree stand. Place the tree stand on the serving table and arrange bags of sugared almonds all around.

Makes 24 small cupcakes

Ingredients

Cupcakes

1 cup cake flour

½ cup ground almonds

1½ teaspoons baking powder

Pinch salt

3½ ounces unsalted butter, room
   temperature

1 cup sugar

1 large egg

1 large egg white

1 teaspoon vanilla extract

½ cup buttermilk

2 tablespoons honey

Almond Frosting (page 17)

Garnish

24 sugared
   almonds

1 Preheat oven to 350°F and line a cupcake pan with paper liners.

2 In a medium bowl, mix together flour, ground almonds, baking powder and salt.

3 In a separate bowl, beat butter and sugar at high speed until light and fluffy.

4 Reduce speed, mix in egg, egg white and vanilla extract.

5 Add flour mixture to butter mixture in 3 batches, alternating with buttermilk and honey, and mixing on low speed after each addition. Beat at high speed for 1 minute until thoroughly combined.

6 Pour batter into cupcake liners until ⅔ full. Bake for about 20 minutes, or until a toothpick inserted in the center comes out clean. Set aside to cool.

7 Frost the cupcakes and garnish with sugared almonds. Serve immediately or refrigerate for up to 2 days in an airtight container.

White Wedding Cupcake Cake

This cake is elegant, exotic, and great for serving at a small family wedding. For best flavor, prepare the coconut lemongrass infusion a night in advance.

Cupcake Cake Idea

● ● ● ● ● ● ● ● ● ● ● ● ● ●

· **3-tier cake stand**
· **Fresh flowers**

Place a single flower on each cupcake and several flowers on the cake. Place the cake on the top tier of the cake stand and place the cupcakes on the middle and bottom tier.

Makes 20 small cupcakes and one 4-inch cake

Ingredients

Cupcakes

1 cup coconut milk

1 lemongrass stick

2 cups cake flour

3 teaspoons baking powder

Pinch salt

3 ounces unsalted butter, room temperature

1½ cups sugar

2 ounces desiccated coconut

2 large eggs

2 large egg whites

2 teaspoons vanilla extract

Frosting

6½ ounces unsalted butter, room temperature

5 cups confectioners' sugar

2 tablespoons coconut milk

2 teaspoons coconut extract

Garnish

20 sugar flowers

Tiny white sprinkles

Cupcakes

1 In a small pan, heat coconut milk and lemongrass over medium heat, then reduce heat to low for about 10 minutes. Do not boil. Remove from heat and set aside to cool. Then refrigerate overnight, leaving the lemongrass in the milk.

2 Preheat oven to 350°F. Line cupcake pans with white paper liners and generously grease a 4-inch cake pan.

3 In a medium bowl, sift together flour, baking powder and salt.

4 In another bowl, mix butter and sugar at high speed for 2 minutes until light and fluffy.

5 Reduce speed. Mix in coconut, eggs, egg whites and vanilla extract.

6 Remove lemongrass stick from milk.

7 Add flour mixture to butter mixture in 3 batches, alternating with lemongrass-infused milk, and mixing on low speed after each addition. Beat at high speed for 1 minute until thoroughly combined.

8 Pour batter into cupcake liners and cake pan until ⅔ full. Bake the cupcakes for about 15 minutes and the cake for about 25 minutes or until a toothpick inserted in the center comes out clean.

Frosting

9 In the bowl of an electric mixer, beat butter, confectioners' sugar, coconut milk and coconut extract at high speed until light and fluffy.

10 Frost the cupcakes and cake then decorate with sugar flowers and white sprinkles. Serve immediately or refrigerate for up to 2 days in an airtight container.

Pomegranate Proposal Cupcake Cake

Add a touch of red to your cupcake cake by using naturally colored foods such as pomegranates and strawberries. If pomegranates are in season, replace the red sprinkles with fresh pomegranate seeds.

Makes 7 regular cupcakes and one 4-inch cake

Ingredients

Cupcakes

¾ cup cake flour

1½ teaspoons baking powder

Pinch salt

1½ ounces unsalted butter, room temperature

¾ cup golden sugar

1 large egg

1 large egg white

1 tablespoon pomegranate syrup

½ cup buttermilk

2 tablespoons strawberry jam

Frosting

3 ounces unsalted butter, room temperature

3 cups confectioners' sugar

1 tablespoon milk

1 tablespoon pomegranate syrup

Garnish

Tiny red sprinkles

Fresh strawberries or pomegranate seeds, optional

Cupcake Cake Idea

• • • • • • • • • • • • • • • •

- **Cake stand**
- **Toothpick***

Place the cake on the cake stand. Insert a toothpick halfway into the center of the cake and gently press on a cupcake. Arrange the other cupcakes all around the cake to create a cupcake flower.

* Remove toothpicks before serving.

Cupcakes

1 Preheat oven to 350°F. Line a cupcake pan with paper liners and generously grease a 4-inch cake pan.

2 In a medium bowl, sift together flour, baking powder and salt.

3 In another bowl, mix butter and sugar at high speed for 2 minutes until light and fluffy.

4 Reduce speed. Add egg, egg white and pomegranate syrup, and mix.

5 Add flour mixture to butter mixture in 3 batches, alternating with buttermilk, and mixing on low speed after each addition. Beat at high speed for 1 minute until thoroughly combined. Fold in the strawberry jam.

6 Pour batter into cupcake liners and cake pan until ⅔ full. Bake the cupcakes for about 15 minutes and the cake for about 25 minutes or until a toothpick inserted in the center comes out clean. Set aside to cool.

Frosting

7 In the bowl of an electric mixer, beat butter, confectioners' sugar and milk until light and fluffy. Mix in the pomegranate syrup until evenly combined.

8 Frost the cupcakes and cake and then top with sprinkles and strawberries or pomegranate seeds. Serve immediately or refrigerate for up to 2 days in an airtight container.

Cupcake Cake Idea

· · · · · · · · · · · · · · · ·

· **White ribbon**
· **2-tier cake stand**

Tie a piece of ribbon around each cupcake and arrange the cupcakes on the cake stand.

Cupcakes

1 Preheat oven to 350°F and line a cupcake pan with paper liners.

2 In a medium bowl, sift together flour, baking powder and salt.

3 In another bowl, mix butter and sugar at high speed for 2 minutes until light and fluffy.

4 Reduce speed. Add egg, egg white and vanilla extract, and mix.

5 Add flour mixture to butter mixture in 3 batches, alternating with buttermilk, and mixing on low speed after each addition. Beat at high speed for 1 minute until thoroughly combined.

6 Pour batter into cupcake liners until ⅔ full. Bake for about 20 minutes, or until a toothpick inserted in the center comes out clean. Set aside to cool.

7 Frost the cupcakes and top with candy pearls and sugar flowers. Serve immediately or refrigerate for up to 2 days in an airtight container.

Wonderland White Cupcake Cake

Here's a classic way to top off a beautiful wedding meal. Frost a batch of white cupcakes with delicate white frosting, wrap them with delicate white ribbons, and decorate with sugar flowers and white sprinkles.

Makes 12 regular cupcakes

Ingredients

Cupcakes

1½ cups cake flour

1½ teaspoons baking powder

Pinch salt

3¼ ounces unsalted butter, room
   temperature

1 cup sugar

1 large egg

1 large egg white

1 teaspoon vanilla extract

½ cup buttermilk

Vanilla Frosting (page 16)

Garnish

Small white candy pearls

Yellow sugar flowers

Cupcake Cake Idea

· ·

- **9 mini cake stands**
- **9 candles**

Place 3 small cupcakes on 8 mini cake stands and arrange the cake stands in a ring on your table.

Place the regular cupcake on the remaining cake stand and place it in the middle of the ring.

Prop a candle in the middle of each trio of cupcakes and insert a candle in the large cupcake in the middle.

1 Preheat oven to 350°F and line a cupcake pan with paper liners.

2 In a medium bowl, sift together flour, baking powder and salt.

3 In a separate bowl, beat butter and sugar at high speed until light and fluffy.

4 Reduce speed and mix in egg, egg white, vanilla extract and cinnamon.

5 Add flour mixture to butter mixture in 3 batches, alternating with buttermilk, and mixing on low speed after each addition. Beat at high speed for 1 minute until thoroughly combined. Fold in the raisins.

6 Pour batter into cupcake liners until ⅔ full. Bake for about 20 minutes or until a toothpick inserted in the center comes out clean. Set aside to cool.

7 Divide the frosting evenly between two bowls and tint one bowl with blue food coloring. Frost half the cupcakes with blue frosting and the other half with white frosting. Sprinkle sugar pearls on all the cupcakes. Serve immediately or refrigerate in an airtight container for up to 2 days.

Happy Hanukkah Cupcake Cake

These sweet cupcakes can be dressed up for any occasion. Serve them in celebration of Hanukkah by topping them with blue and white frosting and sprinkles!

Makes 1 regular cupcake and 24 small cupcakes

Ingredients

Cupcakes

1½ cups cake flour

1½ teaspoons baking powder

Pinch salt

3¼ ounces unsalted butter, room temperature

1 cup brown sugar

1 large egg

1 large egg white

1 teaspoon vanilla extract

1 tablespoon cinnamon

½ cup buttermilk

⅓ cup raisins

Vanilla Frosting (page 16)

Blue food coloring

Garnish

Blue and white sugar pearls

Red Velvet & Blue Cupcake Cake, Fantastic Cran-Tastic Cupcake Cake (page 90) and Chocolate Cheer Cupcake Cake (page 91).

Red Velvet & Blue Cupcake Cake

In this classic recipe, chocolate batter is tinted with red food coloring to create a rich velvety shade of red. As for the cream cheese frosting, it's tinted blue for the holiday.

Makes 24 mini cupcakes

Ingredients

Cupcakes

1 cup cake flour

½ cup cocoa powder

1½ teaspoons baking powder

Pinch salt

3¼ ounces unsalted butter, room temperature

1 cup demerara sugar

1 large egg

1 large egg white

Red food coloring

1 teaspoon vanilla extract

½ cup buttermilk

Cream Cheese Frosting (page 16)

Blue food coloring

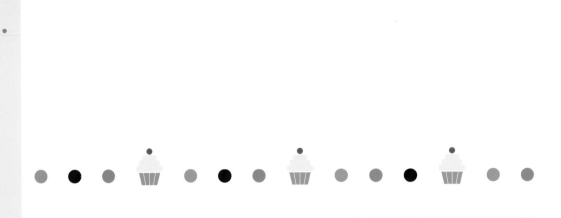

1 Preheat oven to 350°F and line a cupcake pan with paper liners.

2 In a medium bowl, sift together flour, cocoa, baking powder and salt.

3 In a separate bowl, beat butter and sugar at high speed until light and fluffy.

4 Reduce speed and mix in egg, egg white, red food coloring and vanilla extract.

5 Add flour mixture to butter mixture in 3 batches, alternating with buttermilk, and mixing on low speed after each addition. Beat at high speed for 1 minute until thoroughly combined.

6 Pour batter into cupcake liners until ⅔ full and bake for about 18 minutes, or until a toothpick inserted in the center comes out clean. Set aside to cool.

7 Tint the frosting with blue food coloring and then frost the cupcakes. Serve immediately or refrigerate for up to 2 days in an airtight container.

Fantastic Cran-Tastic Cupcake Cake

Cranberries add a tangy tartness to everything they touch. In the giant flag cake (page 86), they provide a pleasant contrast to the sweet chocolate cupcakes.

Makes 24 regular cupcakes

Ingredients

Cupcakes

3 cups cake flour

3 teaspoons baking powder

Pinch salt

6½ ounces unsalted butter, room
   temperature

2 cups sugar

2 large eggs

2 large egg whites

2 teaspoons vanilla extract

1 cup buttermilk

⅔ cup dried cranberries

2 batches Vanilla Frosting (page 16)

1 Preheat oven to 350°F and line a cupcake pan with paper liners.

2 In a medium bowl, sift together flour, baking powder and salt.

3 In a separate bowl, beat butter and sugar at high speed until light and fluffy.

4 Reduce speed and mix in eggs, egg whites and vanilla extract.

5 Add flour mixture to butter mixture in three batches, alternating with buttermilk, and mixing on low speed after each addition. Beat at high speed for 1 minute until thoroughly combined. Fold in the dried cranberries.

6 Frost the cupcakes and serve immediately or refrigerate in airtight container for up to 2 days.

Cupcake Cake Idea

· **Fantastic Cran-Tastic Cupcake Cake**
· **Chocolate Cheer Cupcake Cake** (page 91)
· **Red Velvet & Blue Cupcake Cake** (page 87)
· **Red, white and blue rectangular serving dish**
· **Holiday accessories**

Arrange the cupcakes in a flag design on the serving dish and decorate the table with matching accessories.

Chocolate Cheer Cupcake Cake

These patriotic cupcakes feature an extra big serving of cocoa for even more chocolate goodness. Certain to charm every loyal chocolate lover you know!

Makes 24 regular cupcakes

Ingredients

Cupcakes

2 cups cake flour

1 cup cocoa powder

3 teaspoons baking powder

Pinch salt

6½ ounces unsalted butter, room temperature

2 cups demerara sugar

2 large eggs

2 large egg whites

2 teaspoons vanilla extract

1 cup buttermilk

1 cup milk chocolate chips

Vanilla Frosting (page 16)

Red food coloring

Garnish

White candy stars

Cupcake Cake Idea

- Chocolate Cheer Cupcake Cake
- Fantastic Cran-Tastic Cupcake Cake (page 90)
- Red Velvet & Blue Cupcake Cake (page 87)
- Red, white and blue rectangular serving dish
- Holiday accessories

Arrange the cupcakes in a flag design on the serving dish and decorate the table with matching accessories.

1 Preheat oven to 350°F and line a cupcake pan with paper liners. In a medium bowl, sift together flour, cocoa, baking powder and salt. In a separate bowl, beat butter and sugar at high speed until light and fluffy. Reduce speed and mix in eggs, egg whites and vanilla extract.

2 Add flour mixture to butter mixture in 3 batches, alternating with buttermilk, and mixing on low speed after each addition. Beat for about 1 minute at high speed. Fold in the chocolate chips.

3 Pour batter into cupcake liners until ⅔ full and bake for about 20 minutes or until a toothpick inserted in the center comes out clean. Set aside to cool. Tint the frosting with red food coloring and then frost the cupcakes and sprinkle candy stars on top. Serve immediately or transfer to an airtight container and refrigerate for up to 2 days.

Dandy Brandy Cupcake Cake

Here's a delicious addition to your Christmas dessert table.
For best flavor, soak the raisins in brandy overnight.

**Makes 9 regular cupcakes
and 21 small cupcakes**

Ingredients

Cupcakes

¾ cup raisins

¾ cup brandy

3 cups cake flour

3 teaspoons baking powder

Pinch salt

6½ ounces unsalted butter, room
   temperature

2 cups sugar

2 large eggs

2 large egg whites

2 teaspoons brandy extract

1 cup buttermilk

2 batches Brandy Frosting (page 17)

Green food coloring

Garnish

Christmas candies and sprinkles

• • • • • • • • • • • • • • • •

· Festive placemat or tray

Arrange the cupcakes on the tray so that the regular cupcakes spell out your Christmas message and the small cupcakes are placed all around.

1 Place raisins in a small bowl. Pour in brandy to cover the raisins and soak for 24 hours. Preheat oven to 350°F and line a cupcake pan with paper liners. In a medium bowl, sift together flour, baking powder and salt.

2 In a separate bowl, beat butter and sugar at high speed until light and fluffy.

3 Reduce speed and mix in eggs, egg whites and brandy extract.

4 Add flour mixture to butter mixture in 3 batches, alternating with buttermilk, and mixing on low speed after each addition. Beat at high speed for 1 minute until thoroughly combined.

5 Drain the raisins and fold into cake mixture.

6 Pour batter into cupcake liners until ⅔ full. Bake for about 20 minutes or until a toothpick inserted in the center comes out clean. Set aside to cool.

7 Frost half the regular cupcakes and half the small cupcakes with white frosting, then tint the remaining frosting with green food coloring. Use the green frosting to frost the remaining small cupcakes, and to pipe the letters MERRY XMAS on the regular cupcakes.

8 Decorate all the small cupcakes with Christmas sprinkles. Serve immediately or refrigerate for up to 2 days in an airtight container.

Giant Gingerbread Cupcake Cake

Nothing says Christmas quite like fresh gingerbread. And why limit your options to houses and cookies when you can wow your guests with a giant gingerbread cupcake cake?!

Makes 10 regular cupcakes
and one 5-inch square cake

Ingredients

Cupcakes

2 cups self-rising flour

¾ cup cake flour

½ teaspoon baking soda

4 teaspoons ground ginger

1 teaspoon ground cinnamon

1 teaspoon mixed spices

1 cup brown sugar

3½ ounces unsalted butter, room
   temperature

⅔ cup maple syrup or agave syrup

2 large eggs

1 cup buttermilk

Vanilla Frosting (page 16)

Garnish

Candy-covered chocolates

Christmas candies

Cupcake Cake Idea

· **Rectangular serving dish**

Place the cake at the bottom of the serving dish and arrange the cupcakes in a roof shape above the cake.

1 Preheat oven to 350°F. Line a cupcake pan with paper liners and generously grease a 5-inch square cake pan.

2 In a medium bowl, sift together flour, baking soda, ginger, cinnamon, mixed spice and sugar.

3 Place butter and syrup in saucepan and heat until melted. Set aside to cool.

4 In another bowl, place butter mixture, eggs and buttermilk, and whisk together using a hand whisk.

5 Pour over flour mixture and fold gently until just combined. The batter will be lumpy.

6 Pour batter into cupcake liners and cake pan until ⅔ full. Bake the cupcakes for about 15 minutes and the cake for about 25 minutes until a toothpick inserted in the center comes out clean. Set aside to cool.

7 Frost the cupcakes and cake and decorate with chocolate and Christmas candies. Serve immediately or refrigerate for up to 2 days in an airtight container.

Nutty Noël Cupcake Cake

This richly flavored dessert features cardamom, pistachios and dates. Aromatic and full of flavor, it's an elegant ending for your holiday meal!

Makes 8 regular cupcakes
and one 8-inch cake

Ingredients

Cupcakes

½ cup ground pistachios

½ teaspoon ground cardamom

5½ ounces unsalted butter, room temperature

1½ cups self-rising flour

¾ cup light brown sugar

3 large eggs

½ cup plain yogurt

⅓ cup finely chopped dates

Honey Frosting (page 17)

Garnish

2 tablespoons chopped pistachios

1 Preheat oven to 350°F. Line a cupcake pan with paper liners and generously grease an 8-inch cake pan.

2 In a medium bowl, mix pistachios, cardamom, butter, flour and sugar until combined.

3 Mix in eggs and yogurt until combined. Fold in the chopped dates.

4 Pour batter into cupcake liners and cake pan until ⅔ full. Bake the cupcakes for about 20 minutes and the cake for about 25 minutes, or until a toothpick inserted in the center comes out clean. Set aside to cool.

5 Frost the cupcakes and cake and then sprinkle with chopped pistachios. Serve immediately or refrigerate for up to 2 days in an airtight container.

Cupcake Cake Idea

- Cake stand
- Toothpicks*

Place the cake on the cake stand. Insert a toothpick halfway into the center of the cake and gently press on a cupcake. Affix the rest of the cupcakes to form a circle around the middle cupcake.

* Remove toothpicks before serving.

Happy Holidays Cupcake Cake

If you've maxed out your sweet tooth on chocolate and candies, these cupcakes are a naturally sweet alternative. They feature dates, date honey and poppy seeds.

Cupcake Cake Idea
· · · · · · · · · · · · · · · · · ·
· **Small bowl**
· **Dried fruits and nuts**
· **Large round plate**

Fill the bowl with dried fruits and nuts and place in the middle of a large round plate. Arrange the cupcakes all around.

Makes 15 regular cupcakes

Ingredients

Cupcakes

1½ cups cake flour

1½ teaspoons baking powder

Pinch salt

3 tablespoons poppy seeds

3¼ ounces unsalted butter, room
   temperature

1 cup sugar

1 large egg

1 large egg white

1 teaspoon vanilla extract

½ cup buttermilk

½ cup finely chopped dates

Garnish

2 tablespoons date honey

2 tablespoons poppy seeds

1 Preheat oven to 350°F. Line a cupcake pan with paper liners. In a medium bowl, sift together flour, baking powder and salt. Mix in poppy seeds. In a separate bowl, beat butter and sugar at high speed until light and fluffy. Reduce speed and mix in egg, egg white and vanilla extract.

2 Add flour mixture to butter mixture in three batches, alternating with buttermilk, and mixing on low speed after each addition. Beat at high speed for 1 minute until thoroughly combined. Fold in the dates.

3 Pour batter into cupcake liners until ⅔ full and bake for about 20 minutes, or until a toothpick inserted in the center comes out clean. Set aside to cool.

4 Drizzle date honey on cupcakes and sprinkle poppy seeds on top. Serve immediately or refrigerate for up to 2 days in an airtight container.

Whisky Warm Up Cupcake Cake

Warm up the winter with this delicious combination of whisky and honey. Best served with a glass of warm eggnog or whisky, it's sure to enliven any seasonal celebration.

Makes 12 regular cupcakes and one 8-inch round cake

Ingredients

Cupcakes

3 cups cake flour

3 teaspoons baking powder

Pinch salt

6½ ounces unsalted butter, room temperature

2 cups brown sugar

2 large eggs

2 large egg whites

2 teaspoons vanilla extract

1 cup buttermilk

¼ cup honey

Frosting

6 ounces unsalted butter, room temperature

6 cups confectioners' sugar

3 tablespoons Irish cream whisky (such as Bailey's Irish Cream)

Garnish

Silver sprinkles

Cupcake Cake Idea

· Holiday ribbon
· 14-inch metal cake stand

Wrap a piece of holiday ribbon around the base of the stand. Place the cake on the cake stand and arrange the cupcakes all around the cake.

Cupcakes

1 Preheat oven to 350°F. Line a cupcake pan with metallic green liners and generously grease an 8-inch round cake pan. In a medium bowl, sift together flour, baking powder and salt.

2 In a separate bowl, beat butter and sugar at high speed until light and fluffy.

3 Reduce speed and mix in eggs, egg whites and vanilla extract.

4 Add flour mixture to butter mixture in 3 batches, alternating with buttermilk, and mixing on low speed after each addition. Beat at high speed for 1 minute until thoroughly combined. Fold in the honey.

5 Pour batter into cupcake liners and cake pan until ⅔ full. Bake the cupcakes for about 15 minutes and the cake for about 25 minutes until a toothpick inserted in the center comes out clean. Set aside to cool.

Frosting

6 In the bowl of an electric mixer, beat butter, confectioners' sugar and whisky at high speed until light and fluffy.

7 Frost the cupcakes and cakes and then decorate with metallic silver sprinkles. Serve immediately or refrigerate for up to 2 days in an airtight container.

Lucky Lemon Cupcake Cake and Think! Pink! Cupcake Cake (page 106)

Lucky Lemon Cupcake Cake

This recipe makes the most of three distinct flavors: creamy white chocolate, tangy lemon and nutty coconut. It's a great base for showing off Easter cupcakes.

Makes one 6-inch round cake

Ingredients

Cupcakes

⅕ cup cake flour

1½ teaspoons baking powder

Pinch salt

3¼ ounces unsalted butter, room temperature

1 cup sugar

1 large egg

1 large egg white

1 teaspoon lemon extract

1 tablespoon lemon zest

½ cup buttermilk

½ cup white chocolate chips

Lemon Frosting (page 17)

Garnish

½ cup coconut flakes

Cupcake Cake Idea
. . . .

- **Lucky Lemon Cupcake Cake**
- **Think! Pink! Cupcake Cake**
(page 106)
- **Cake stand and matching plate**
- **Toothpicks***

Place the cake on the cake stand. Pierce 3 cupcakes with toothpicks and position them in a ring on the top of the cake. Place the rest of the cupcakes on the matching plate.

* Remove toothpicks before serving.

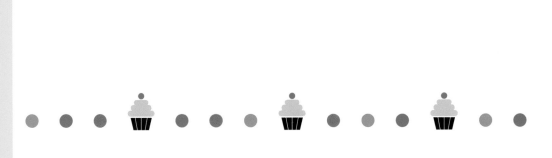

1 Preheat oven to 350°F and generously grease a 6-inch cake pan.

2 In a medium bowl, sift together flour, baking powder and salt.

3 In a separate bowl, beat butter and sugar at high speed until light and fluffy. Reduce speed and mix in egg, egg white, lemon extract and lemon zest.

4 Add flour mixture to butter mixture in 3 batches, alternating with buttermilk, and mixing on low speed after each addition. Beat at high speed for 1 minute until thoroughly combined. Fold in the chocolate chips until evenly combined.

5 Pour batter into cake pan until ⅔ full. Bake for about 30 minutes or until a toothpick inserted in the center comes out clean. Set aside to cool.

6 Frost the cake and sprinkle with coconut flakes. Serve immediately or refrigerate for up to 2 days in an airtight container.

Lucky Lemon Cupcake Cake (page 103) and Think! Pink! Cupcake Cake (page 106)

Think! Pink! Cupcake Cake

These versatile cupcakes can be topped with any type of Easter treat that you like. Decorate with pastel colored chocolate eggs, jelly beans or sugared almonds.

Makes 12 regular cupcakes

Cupcake Cake Idea

· **Lucky Lemon Cupcake Cake** (page 103)
· **Think! Pink! Cupcake Cake**
· **Cake stand and matching plate**
· **Toothpicks***

Place the cake on the cake stand. Pierce 3 cupcakes with toothpicks and position them in a ring on the top of the cake. Place the rest of the cupcakes on the matching plate.

* Remove toothpicks before serving.

Ingredients

Cupcakes

1½ cups cake flour

2 tablespoons cinnamon

1½ teaspoons baking powder

Pinch salt

3¼ ounces unsalted butter, room temperature

1 cup superfine sugar

1 large egg

1 large egg white

1 teaspoon vanilla extract

½ cup buttermilk

Vanilla Frosting (page 16)

Pink food coloring

Garnish

12 mini Easter eggs

1 Preheat oven to 350°F and line a cupcake pan with paper liners.

2 In a medium bowl, sift together flour, cinnamon, baking powder and salt.

3 In a separate bowl, beat butter and sugar at high speed until light and fluffy. Reduce speed and mix in egg, egg white and vanilla extract.

4 Add flour mixture to butter mixture in 3 batches, alternating with buttermilk, and mixing on low speed after each addition. Beat at high speed for 1 minute until thoroughly combined.

5 Pour batter into cupcake liners until ⅔ full. Bake for about 20 minutes, or until a toothpick inserted in the center comes out clean. Set aside to cool.

6 Tint the frosting with pink food coloring and then frost the cupcakes. Top each cupcake with a mini Easter egg. Serve immediately or refrigerate in an airtight container for up to 2 days.

Charming Chai Cupcake Cake

Sweeten up Easter brunch by serving this delicate cupcakes.
If you can't find agave syrup at your local store, substitute with
natural honey.

Cupcake Cake Idea

· · · · · · · · · · · · · · · ·

- **6 tea cups**
- **6 tea saucers**

Arrange the tea cups and saucers on your table and place a cupcake on each one.

Makes 12 regular cupcakes

Ingredients

Cupcakes

3 chai tea bags
⅔ cup boiling water
¼ cup agave syrup
2 ounces unsalted butter, melted
¼ cup buttermilk
1 large egg
1½ cups all-purpose flour
1 cup brown sugar
1 teaspoon baking soda
¼ teaspoon salt
Cream Cheese Frosting (page 16)

Garnish

¼ cup agave syrup

1 Place the tea bags in a tea cup and pour in boiling water. Let tea steep for about 15 minutes, then remove teabags and set tea aside to cool.

2 Preheat oven to 350°F and line a cupcake pan with paper liners.

3 In a medium bowl, mix agave syrup, butter, buttermilk and egg on medium speed until combined.

4 Sift flour into a separate bowl, and combine with brown sugar, baking soda and salt. Mix flour into buttermilk mixture until combined, and then fold in the tea.

5 Pour batter into cupcake liners until ⅔ full and bake for about 20 minutes, or until a toothpick inserted in the center comes out clean. Set aside to cool.

6 Frost the cupcakes and drizzle agave syrup on top. Serve immediately or refrigerate for up to 2 days in an airtight container.

Marvelously Maple Cupcake Cake

Serving pancakes at Easter brunch? How about serving these pancake-inspired cupcakes too! Include maple syrup in the batter, then drizzle on top before serving.

Cupcake Cake Idea

· **Cherry Blossom Cupcake Cake** (page 109)
· **Marvelously Maple Cupcake Cake**
· **2-tier cake stand**

Place the cake on the top tier of the cake stand and arrange the cupcakes on the bottom tier.

Makes 24 mini cupcakes

Ingredients

Cupcakes

1¼ cups cake flour

1½ teaspoons baking powder

Pinch salt

2 ounces unsalted butter, room temperature

¾ cup brown sugar

1 large egg

1 large egg white

1 teaspoon vanilla extract

⅜ cup buttermilk

⅛ cup maple syrup, plus more for drizzling

1 Preheat oven to 350°F and line a cupcake pan with paper liners.

2 In a medium bowl, sift together flour, baking powder and salt.

3 In a separate bowl, beat butter and sugar at high speed until light and fluffy.

4 Reduce speed and mix in egg, egg white and vanilla extract.

5 In a small cup, combine buttermilk with maple syrup.

6 Add flour mixture to butter mixture in 3 batches, alternating with buttermilk mixture, and mixing on low speed after each addition. Beat at high speed for 1 minute until thoroughly combined.

7 Pour batter into cupcake liners until ⅔ full and bake for about 16 minutes, or until a toothpick inserted in the center comes out clean. Set aside to cool.

8 Drizzle maple syrup on the cupcakes then serve immediately or refrigerate for up to 2 days in an airtight container.

Cherry Blossom Cupcake Cake

Delicately pink blossoming almond and cherry trees are sure signs of spring. Top these almond cherry cupcakes with pink sprinkles for a pretty Easter dessert.

Makes one 7-inch round cake

Ingredients

Cupcakes

1⅓ cups cake flour

1½ teaspoons baking powder

⅓ cup ground almonds

Pinch salt

3¼ ounces unsalted butter, room
   temperature

1 cup light brown sugar

1 large egg

1 large egg white

1 teaspoon vanilla extract

½ cup buttermilk

⅓ cup frozen pitted cherries, thawed
   and strained

Almond Frosting (page 17)

Pink food coloring

Garnish

Pink sprinkles

Cupcake Cake Idea

· **Cherry Blossom Cupcake Cake**
· **Marvelously Maple Cupcake
Cake** (page 108)
· **2-tier cake stand**

Place the cake on the top tier of the cake stand and arrange the cupcakes on the bottom tier.

1 Preheat oven to 350°F and generously grease a 7-inch round cake pan. In a medium bowl, sift together flour, baking powder, almonds and salt. In a separate bowl, beat butter and sugar at high speed until light and fluffy.

2 Reduce speed and mix in egg, egg white and vanilla extract.

3 Add flour mixture to butter mixture in 3 batches, alternating with buttermilk, and mixing on low speed after each addition. Beat at high speed for 1 minute until thoroughly combined. Fold in the cherries.

4 Pour batter into cake pan until ⅔ full and bake for about 35 minutes or until a toothpick inserted in the center comes out clean. Set aside to cool.

5 Tint the frosting with pink food coloring and then frost the cake and decorate with pink sprinkles. Serve immediately or refrigerate for up to 2 days in an airtight container.

Bunny Knows Best Cupcake Cake

Treat the Easter bunny to nutty carrot cupcakes topped with creamy frosting. You'll have all the Easter bunnies you know hoppingly happy and asking for seconds!

Cupcake Cake Idea

· **Orange and green food coloring**

To make a carrot shaped cupcake cake, tint ⅔ of the frosting orange and the rest green. Frost 10 cupcakes with orange frosting and arrange in a carrot shape. Frost the other 5 cupcakes with green frosting and arrange at the top of the carrot.

Makes 15 regular cupcakes

Ingredients

Cupcakes
½ cup finely grated carrot
1½ cups cake flour
2 teaspoons cinnamon
1½ teaspoons baking powder
Pinch salt
3¼ ounces unsalted butter, room temperature
1 cup light brown sugar
1 large egg
1 teaspoon vanilla extract
½ cup buttermilk

¼ cup raisins
¼ cup chopped walnuts
Cream Cheese Frosting (page 16)

Garnish
15 walnut halves

1 Preheat oven to 350°F and line a cupcake pan with paper liners. Place grated carrot in a strainer and set aside to let excess water drain while you prepare the batter.

2 In the meantime, sift together flour, cinnamon, baking powder and salt in a medium bowl. In a separate bowl, beat butter and sugar at high speed until light and fluffy. Reduce speed and mix in egg and vanilla extract.

3 Add flour mixture to butter mixture in 3 batches, alternating with buttermilk, and mixing on low speed after each addition. Beat at high speed for 1 minute until thoroughly combined. Fold in the grated carrot, raisins and chopped walnuts until evenly combined.

4 Pour batter into cupcake pan until ⅔ full. Bake for about 20 minutes or until a toothpick inserted in the center comes out clean. Set aside to cool. Frost the cupcakes and then garnish with walnuts. Serve immediately or refrigerate for up to 2 days in an airtight container.

Easy Easter Cheesecake Cupcake Cake

Celebrate the spring with these miniature cheesecakes. They have a crunchy oatmeal bottom, smooth fruity topping and are remarkable easy to make!

Makes 12 regular cupcakes

Ingredients

Cupcakes

1 pound cream cheese, room
  temperature

½ cup sugar

1 teaspoon vanilla extract

2 large eggs

½ cup sour cream

Pinch salt

15 oatmeal cookies, crushed

Passion Fruit Coulis

8 passion fruit

¾ cup sugar

Juice of ½ lemon

Cupcake Cake Idea

· Wicker basket
· Pastel colored jelly beans or chocolate eggs

Fill the basket with the jelly beans or chocolate eggs and arrange the cupcakes all around the basket.

Cupcakes

1 Preheat oven to 350°F and line a cupcake pan with paper liners. In a medium bowl, beat cream cheese at medium-high speed until smooth. Beat in sugar until combined, and then mix in the vanilla. In a small bowl, beat the eggs and then gradually add to cream cheese mixture until combined. Mix in sour cream and salt.

2 Distribute crushed oatmeal cookie crumbs evenly among the cupcake liners and press into the bottom. Add batter until cupcake liners are full.

3 Bake for 10 minutes, then rotate pan 180° and bake for 10 more minutes, until the filling sets. Transfer to a wire rack and set aside to cool, and then refrigerate for at least 4 hours.

Coulis

4 Cut passion fruit in half, scoop out insides and transfer to a small saucepan. Mix in the sugar and lemon and bring to a boil, then reduce heat and simmer for about 5 minutes, until texture thickens. Drizzle warm coulis over the cupcakes. Serve immediately or refrigerate for up to 2 days in an airtight container.

Boo-berry Vanilla Cupcake Cake

Scare up some smiles with this delicious spotty treats. Blueberries are a fun and healthy alternative to chocolate chips…and they taste delicious too! Top these cupcakes with a fun colorful frosting to suit any occasion!

Makes 12 regular cupcakes and one 5-inch square cake

Ingredients

Cupcakes

3 cups cake flour

3 teaspoons baking powder

Pinch salt

6½ ounces unsalted butter, room temperature

2 cups sugar

2 large eggs

2 teaspoons vanilla extract

1 cup buttermilk

1 cup blueberries

3 batches Vanilla Frosting (page 16)

Black food coloring

Green food coloring

Garnish

Orange sprinkles

Cupcake Cake Idea

· **Square serving tray**
· **Decorative holiday toothpicks**

Place the cake on the serving tray and arrange cupcakes all around. Scatter a few holiday toothpicks on the tray.

1 Preheat oven to 350°F. Line a cupcake pan with paper liners and generously grease a 5-inch square cake pan. In a medium bowl, sift together flour, baking powder and salt. In a separate bowl, beat butter and sugar at high speed until light and fluffy. Reduce speed and mix in eggs and vanilla extract.

2 Add flour mixture to butter mixture in 3 batches, alternating with buttermilk, and mixing on low speed after each addition. Beat at high speed for 1 minute until thoroughly combined. Fold in the blueberries.

3 Pour batter into cupcake liners and cake pan until ⅔ full. Bake the cupcakes for about 15 minutes and the cake for about 25 minutes until a toothpick inserted in the center comes out clean. Set aside to cool.

4 Divide the frosting between three bowls. Tint ⅓ of the frosting with black food coloring, leave 3 tablespoons white, and tint the rest with green food coloring.

5 Frost the cupcakes with green frosting and sprinkle with orange sprinkles. Frost the cake with black frosting and use white frosting to write a holiday message. Serve immediately or transfer to an airtight container and refrigerate for up to 2 days.

Spider Web Cupcake Cake

Even arachnophobes will get a kick out of this cupcake cake!
It's fun to decorate, a pleasure to serve and a delight to eat!

Makes 15 regular cupcakes

Ingredients

Cupcakes

1⅓ cups cake flour

½ cup cocoa powder

1½ teaspoons baking powder

Pinch salt

½ cup unsalted butter, room
   temperature

1 cup dark brown sugar

1 large egg

1 large egg white

1 teaspoon vanilla extract

½ cup buttermilk

Frosting

4 cups + 1 cup confectioners' sugar

5 tablespoons warm water

1 teaspoon vanilla extract

Black food coloring

2 tablespoons butter

White food coloring

Cupcake Cake Idea

- Cake stand
- Halloween-themed napkins
- Candy spiders
- Black licorice candies

Line the cake stand with napkins and arrange the cupcakes on top. Place candy spiders on each cupcake and decorate the cake stand with black licorice.

Cupcakes

1 Preheat oven to 350°F and line a cupcake pan with paper liners.

2 In a medium bowl, sift together flour, cocoa, baking powder and salt.

3 In a separate bowl, beat butter and sugar at high speed until light and fluffy.

4 Reduce speed and mix in egg, egg white and vanilla extract.

5 Add flour mixture to butter mixture in three batches, alternating with buttermilk, and mixing on low speed after each addition.

6 Beat at high speed for 1 minute until thoroughly combined.

7 Pour batter into cupcake pan until full. Bake for about 15 minutes or until a toothpick inserted in the center comes out clean. Set aside to cool.

Frosting

8 Place 4 cups of confectioners' sugar in a bowl. Add warm water slowly while mixing until mixture turns from thick paste to liquid.

9 Continue mixing and add vanilla extract and a few drops of black food coloring.

10 Quickly pour mixture on the cupcakes, filling cups to the rim, and then set aside to set.

11 In a separate bowl, mix remaining 1 cup of confectioners' sugar, butter and white food coloring, until a paste forms.

12 Transfer mixture to a pastry bag fitted with a fine writing nozzle. Draw spider's webs on each cupcake by making 3 hexagon shapes, one inside the other, and joining them with straight lines at each corner. Serve immediately or refrigerate for up to 2 days in an airtight container.

Donut Delight Cupcake Cake

People tend to eat jelly filled donuts on Hannukah, but that's not to say you can't indulge in some chocolate-glazed ones as well. Create a giant chocolate glazed donut with a dozen of these fun cupcakes.

Makes 12 regular cupcakes

Ingredients

Cupcakes

1½ cups cake flour

1½ teaspoons baking powder

Pinch salt

3¼ ounces unsalted butter, room
    temperature

1 cup sugar

1 large egg

1 large egg white

1 teaspoon vanilla or strawberry extract

½ cup buttermilk

Chocolate Glaze

4 ounces dark chocolate, chopped

1 teaspoon vanilla extract

1 tablespoon corn syrup

⅔ cup double cream

1 cup sugar

Garnish

Rainbow sprinkles

Cupcake Cake Idea

• • • • • • • • • • • • • •

· **Round tray**

Arrange the cupcakes in a donut shape by placing them in a ring around the edges of the tray. Leave the middle of the tray empty.

Cupcakes

1 Preheat oven to 350°F and line a cupcake pan with paper liners.

2 In a medium bowl, sift together flour, baking powder and salt.

3 In a separate bowl, beat butter and sugar at high speed until light and fluffy. Reduce speed and mix in egg, egg white and extract.

4 Add flour mixture to butter mixture in 3 batches, alternating with buttermilk, and mixing on low speed after each addition. Beat at high speed for 1 minute until thoroughly combined.

5 Pour batter into cupcake liners until ⅔ full. Bake for about 20 minutes or until a toothpick inserted in the center comes out clean. Set aside to cool.

6 With a sharp knife, carefully remove the core of the cupcakes and arrange them on a baking sheet.

Glaze

7 Place chocolate, vanilla and corn syrup in small heatproof bowl.

8 In a small saucepan over medium heat, heat cream and sugar.

9 Pour cream mixture into bowl with chocolate and let it sit for a few minutes, and then mix until smooth.

10 Pour mixture over cupcakes, covering tops completely and letting the glaze drip down the sides. Decorate with rainbow sprinkles. Serve immediately or transfer to an airtight container and refrigerate until ready to serve.

Golden Raisin Cupcake Cake

Celebrate the Festival of Lights with this golden cupcake cake. In addition to golden raisins, it also includes creamy chocolate chips and nutty almonds.

Makes 12 regular cupcakes

Ingredients

Cupcakes

1½ cups cake flour

1½ teaspoons baking powder

Pinch salt

3¼ cups unsalted butter, room temperature

1 cup light brown sugar

1 large egg

1 large egg white

1 teaspoon almond extract

½ cup buttermilk

⅓ cup golden raisins

½ cup milk chocolate chips

Almond Frosting (page 17)

Garnish

Chocolate curls

Cupcake Cake Idea

· · · · · · · · · · · · · · · · · · ·

· **Toothpicks***
· **Candles**

Create a cupcake menorah by arranging 9 cupcakes in a row. Insert a toothpick in the middle of the 5th cupcake in the row and press on a cupcake, so that the middle cupcake is actually a double cupcake. Insert candles into each cupcake.

***Remove toothpicks before serving.**

1 Preheat oven to 350°F. Line a cupcake pan with paper liners. In a medium bowl, sift together flour, baking powder and salt. In a separate bowl, beat butter and sugar at high speed until light and fluffy. Reduce speed and mix in egg, egg white and almond extract.

2 Add flour mixture to butter mixture in 3 batches, alternating with buttermilk, and mixing on low speed after each addition. Beat at high speed for 1 minute until thoroughly combined. Fold in the raisins and chocolate chips.

3 Pour batter into cupcake liners until ⅔ full. Bake for about 15 minutes or until a toothpick inserted in the center comes out clean. Set aside to cool.

4 Frost the cupcakes and decorate with chocolate curls. Serve immediately or refrigerate for up to 2 days in an airtight container.

Chocolate Coin Cupcake Cake

Chocolate coins are a favorite Hannukah treat, so they're perfect for topping a plate full of cupcakes. Have plenty of extra chocolate coins on hand, to decorate your dessert table and keep hungry fingers at bay!

Makes 18 small cupcakes

Ingredients

Cupcakes

1½ cups cake flour

1½ teaspoons baking powder

Pinch salt

3¼ ounces unsalted butter, room temperature

1 cup demerara sugar

1 large egg

1 large egg white

1 teaspoon vanilla extract

½ cup buttermilk

Frosting

2 ounces milk chocolate, chopped

3¼ ounces unsalted butter, room temperature

2½ cups confectioners' sugar

3 tablespoons milk

Garnish

12 chocolate coins

Cupcake Cake Idea
. . . .
- **Rectangular tray**
- **Extra gold coins**

Arrange the cupcakes on the tray and arrange the chocolate coins all around.

Cupcakes

1 Preheat oven to 350°F. Line a cupcake pan with paper liners and generously grease a 4-inch round cake pan. In a medium bowl, sift together flour, baking powder and salt. In a separate bowl, beat butter and sugar at high speed until light and fluffy. Reduce speed and mix in egg, egg white and vanilla extract.

2 Add flour mixture to butter mixture in 3 batches, alternating with buttermilk, and mixing on low speed after each addition. Beat at high speed for 1 minute until thoroughly combined.

3 Pour batter into cupcake and cake pan until ⅔ full. Bake the cupcakes for 15 minutes and the cake for 25 minutes, or until a toothpick inserted in the center comes out clean. Set aside to cool.

Frosting

4 Melt chocolate in the top of a double boiler, and then set aside to cool until warm to the touch. In the bowl of an electric mixer, beat butter, confectioners' sugar and milk at high speed until light and fluffy. Fold in the melted chocolate. Frost the cupcakes and cake and then top each cupcake with a chocolate coin. Serve immediately or refrigerate for up to 2 days in an airtight container.

The Great Pumpkin Cupcake Cake

Spice up your Thanksgiving dessert table with this giant cupcake. If you don't have rolled fondant to make the stem, substitute with a green pipe cleaner.

Makes one 8½ x 15½-inch cupcake

Ingredients

Cupcakes

3 cups canned pumpkin purée

3¾ cups brown sugar

1½ cups vegetable oil

6 large eggs

4 cups cake flour

3 teaspoons baking powder

1½ teaspoons baking soda

Pinch salt

3 teaspoons ground cinnamon

1½ teaspoons ground ginger

1 teaspoon allspice

1 cup raisins

2 batches Vanilla Frosting (page 16)

Orange food coloring

Brown food coloring

Green food coloring

1 tablespoon rolled fondant (sugar dough)

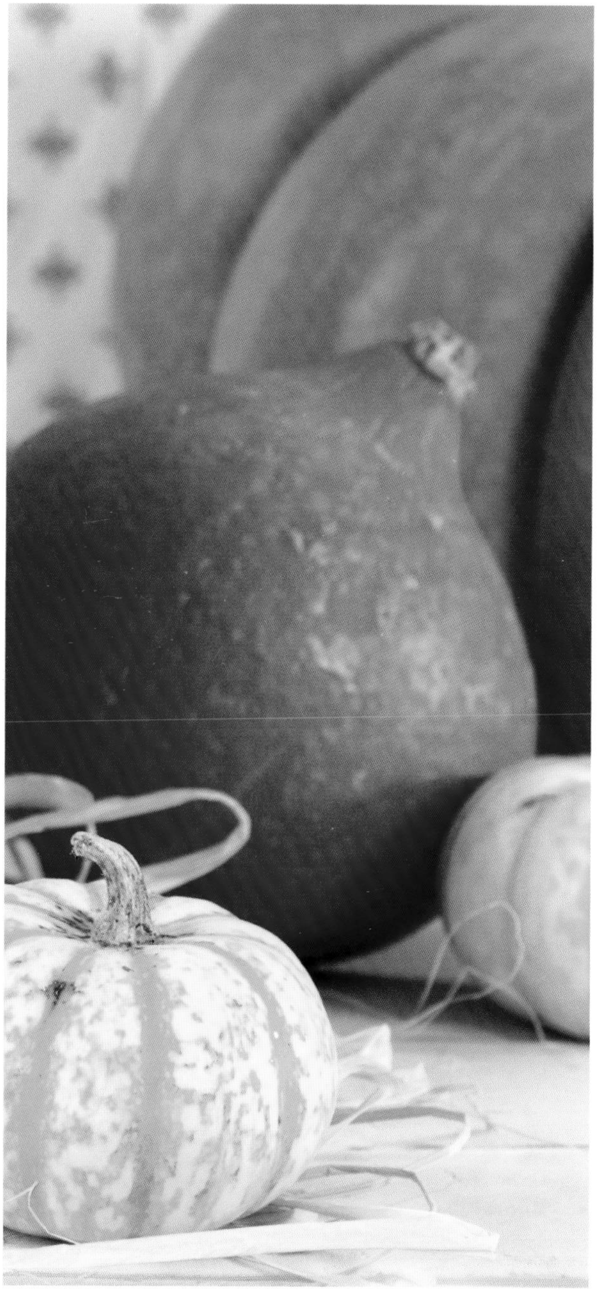

Cupcake Cake Idea

• • • • • • • • • • • • • • • •

- **Bamboo ribbon**
- **Cake stand**
- **Gourds, mini pumpkins, and other autumn accessories**

Tie a piece of bamboo ribbon around the base of the cupcake and place the cupcake on the cake stand. Decorate the table with Thanksgiving decorations such as gourds and mini pumpkins.

1 Preheat oven to 350°F and generously grease an 8½ x 15½-inch giant cupcake pan.

2 In a medium bowl, whisk together pumpkin purée, sugar, oil and eggs.

3 Add flour, baking powder, baking soda, salt, cinnamon, ginger and allspice, and whisk until combined. Fold in the raisins.

4 Pour batter into cake pan until ⅔ full and bake for about 35 minutes, or until a toothpick inserted in the center comes out clean. Set aside to cool.

5 Divide the frosting evenly between 2 bowls. Tint one half of the frosting with orange food coloring and the other half with brown.

6 Frost the bottom half of the cake with brown frosting and the top half with orange frosting, then put the two cakes together to make a giant cupcake.

7 Tint the rolled fondant with green food coloring, shape it into a stem shape and insert it at the top of the cupcake. Serve immediately or transfer to an airtight container and refrigerate for up to 2 days.

Cinn-apple Cinna-bration Cupcake Cake

Celebrate the apple harvest on Thanksgiving with this enticing recipe. After all, few things are as tantalizing as the scent of freshly apples baked with cinnamon.

Makes 24 mini cupcakes

Cupcake Cake Idea

· **Round serving tray**
· **Toothpicks***

Create a double-decker cupcake cake by arranging 17 cupcakes in a circle on the base of the tray. Stack the other cupcakes on top. Use toothpicks to affix if necessary.

* Remove toothpicks before serving.

Ingredients

Cupcakes

1½ cups cake flour

1½ teaspoons baking powder

1½ tablespoons cinnamon

Pinch salt

3¼ ounces unsalted butter, room temperature

1 cup light brown sugar

1 large egg

1 large egg white

1 teaspoon vanilla extract

½ cup buttermilk

¾ cup finely diced apple

Creamy Caramel (page 18)

1 Preheat oven to 350°F and line a cupcake pan with paper liners.

2 In a medium bowl, sift together flour, baking powder, cinnamon and salt.

3 In a separate bowl, beat butter and sugar at high speed until light and fluffy.

4 Reduce speed and mix in egg, egg white and vanilla extract.

5 Add flour mixture to butter mixture in 3 batches, alternating with buttermilk, and mixing on low speed after each addition. Beat at high speed for 1 minute until thoroughly combined. Fold in the diced apple.

6 Pour batter into cupcake pan until ⅔ full and bake for about 20 minutes or until a toothpick inserted in the center comes out clean.

7 Drizzled warm cupcakes with caramel. Serve immediately or refrigerate for up to 2 days in an airtight container.

Thankful Medley Cupcake Cake

Add a Mediterranean touch to your Thanksgiving offerings with this flavorful cupcake. It features rosewater, pistachios and Turkish Delight, as well as a smooth white chocolate frosting.

Makes 12 regular cupcakes

Ingredients

Cupcakes
1½ cups cake flour

1½ teaspoons baking powder

Pinch salt

3¼ ounces unsalted butter, room
    temperature

1 cup light brown sugar

1 large egg

1 large egg white

2 tablespoons rosewater

1 teaspoon vanilla extract

½ cup buttermilk

2 tablespoons chopped pistachios

Rich Chocolate Frosting (page 17) made
    with white chocolate chips

Garnish
½ cup chopped Turkish Delight

Cupcake Cake Idea

· **2-tier cake stand**
· **Cellophane wrapper**
· **Ribbon**

Arrange the cupcakes on both layers of the cake stand.
Wrap the stand with cellophane and decorate with a festive ribbon.

1 Preheat oven to 350°F and line a cupcake pan with paper liners. In a medium bowl, sift together flour, baking powder and salt. In a separate bowl, beat butter and sugar at high speed until light and fluffy.

2 Reduce speed and mix in egg, egg white, rosewater and vanilla extract.

3 Add flour mixture to butter mixture in 3 batches, alternating with buttermilk, and mixing on low speed after each addition. Beat at high speed for 1 minute until thoroughly combined. Fold in the pistachios.

4 Pour batter into cupcake pan until ⅔ full. Bake for about 20 minutes or until a toothpick inserted in the center comes out clean. Set aside to cool.

5 Frost the cupcakes and decorate with pieces of Turkish Delight. Serve immediately or refrigerate for up to 2 days in an airtight container.

In Praise of Pecans Cupcake Cake

This twist on the traditional Thanksgiving pecan pie includes sugared pecans both inside and out, and a sweet honey frosting. If you like, substitute the pecans with sugared almonds or peanuts.

Makes 12 regular cupcakes

Cupcake Cake Idea
● ● ● ● ● ● ● ● ● ● ● ● ● ● ●
· **Large round plate**
· **Small pot of honey**

Place the honey pot in the middle of the plate. Arrange the cupcakes all around.

Ingredients

Cupcakes

1½ cups cake flour

1½ teaspoons baking powder

Pinch salt

3¼ ounces unsalted butter, room temperature

1 cup light brown sugar

1 large egg

1 large egg white

1 teaspoon vanilla extract

½ cup buttermilk

½ cup chopped sugared pecans

Honey Frosting (page 17)

Garnish

12 sugared pecans

1 Preheat oven to 350°F and line a cupcake pan with paper liners. In a medium bowl, sift together flour, baking powder and salt. In a separate bowl, beat butter and sugar at high speed until light and fluffy. Reduce speed and mix in egg, egg white and vanilla extract.

2 Add flour mixture to butter mixture in 3 batches, alternating with buttermilk, and mixing on low speed after each addition. Beat at high speed for 1 minute until thoroughly combined. Fold in the chopped sugared pecans.

3 Pour batter into cupcake pan until ⅔ full. Bake for about 20 minutes, or until a toothpick inserted in the center comes out clean. Set aside to cool.

4 Frost the cupcakes and garnish each with a sugared pecan. Serve immediately or refrigerate for up to 2 days in an airtight container.

Almond Pear-fection Cupcake Cake

These light cupcakes are a perfect finish to a satisfying Thanksgiving meal. They include fresh autumn fruit, nutty ground almonds, and creamy chocolate ganâche.

Makes 48 mini cupcakes

Ingredients

Cupcakes

3 large pears, peeled, cored and chopped into small chunks

1½ cups ground almonds

1 cup sugar

1 teaspoon baking powder

1 teaspoon vanilla extract

6 eggs

Chocolate Ganâche (page 18)

Garnish

⅓ cup flaked almonds

1 Preheat oven to 350°F and line a cupcake pan with paper liners.

2 Place pears in a medium pot and add water to cover. Bring the water to a boil over medium heat, and then reduce heat to low and simmer for about 25 minutes, until soft.

3 Remove pears from the water with a slotted spoon and set aside to cool. Then transfer to a food processor and blend until smooth.

4 Transfer to the bowl of an electric mixer. Add ground almonds, sugar, baking powder and vanilla, and mix until just combined.

5 Mix in eggs until combined.

6 Pour batter into cupcake liners until ⅔ full and bake for about 15 minutes, until golden and firm. Set aside to cool.

7 Drizzle with chocolate ganâche and decorate with flaked almonds. Serve immediately or refrigerate for up to 2 days in an airtight container.

Cupcake Cake Idea

• • • • • • • • • • • • • • •

· 3-tier cupcake stand

Arrange the cupcakes on each of the tiers on the cupcake stand.

Radiant Roses Cupcake Cake

Who doesn't love roses on Valentine's Day?
If you've never made flowers with frosting before, practice on a
piece of waxed paper first.

Makes 12 regular cupcakes

Ingredients

Cupcakes

1¼ cups cake flour

½ cup cocoa powder

1½ teaspoons baking powder

Pinch salt

3¼ ounces unsalted butter, room
   temperature

1 cup brown sugar

1 large egg

1 large egg white

½ cup buttermilk

Cherry Frosting (page 17)

Cupcake Cake Idea

- **1 jug**
- **1 piece floral foam**
- **12 wooden skewers***

Tuck the foam into the jug and the wooden skewers. Arrange them as you like and make sure they are secure in the foam. Press a cupcake onto the top of each skewer so that it is securely in place. Make sure the skewer doesn't poke out the top of the cupcake.

***Remove skewers before serving.**

1 Preheat oven to 350°F and line a cupcake pan with gold metallic liners.

2 In a medium bowl, sift together flour, cocoa, baking powder and salt.

3 In a separate bowl, beat butter and sugar at high speed until light and fluffy.

4 Reduce speed and mix in egg and egg white.

5 Add flour mixture to butter mixture in 3 batches, alternating with buttermilk, and mixing on low speed after each addition. Beat at high speed for 1 minute until thoroughly combined.

6 Pour batter into cupcake liners until ⅔ full. Bake for about 20 minutes, or until a toothpick inserted in the center comes out clean. Set aside to cool.

7 Frost the cupcakes and serve immediately or refrigerate for up to 2 days in an airtight container.

Box of Chocolates Cupcake Cake

Boxed chocolates are a Valentine's Day staple. For a lovely cupcake variation, bake a dozen Belgian-style cupcakes and serve in a box wrapped with love!

Makes 12 regular cupcakes

Ingredients

Cupcakes

1⅓ cups cake flour

½ cup cocoa powder

1½ teaspoons baking powder

Pinch salt

3¼ ounces unsalted butter, room temperature

1 cup demerara sugar

1 large egg

1 large egg white

1 teaspoon vanilla extract

½ cup buttermilk

⅓ cup chopped Belgian chocolate or Belgian chocolate chips

Garnish

Red candy hearts

1 Preheat oven to 350°F and line a cupcake pan with paper liners.

2 In a medium bowl, sift together flour, cocoa, baking powder and salt.

3 In a separate bowl, beat butter and sugar at high speed until light and fluffy.

4 Reduce speed and mix in egg, egg white and vanilla extract.

5 Add flour mixture to butter mixture in 3 batches, alternating with buttermilk, and mixing on low speed after each addition. Beat at high speed for 1 minute until thoroughly combined. Fold in the chocolate chips.

6 Pour batter into cupcake pan until ⅔ full. Bake for about 20 minutes or until a toothpick inserted in the center comes out clean. Set aside to cool.

7 Frost the cupcakes and sprinkle with red hearts. Serve immediately or refrigerate for up to 2 days in an airtight container.

Ode to Oranges Cupcake Cake

If the person you're crazy about isn't crazy about chocolate, this citrus cupcake is sure to delight. Fresh and refreshing, serve it with fragrant herbal tea.

Makes 6 small cupcakes and one 6-inch round cake

Ingredients

Cupcakes

1½ cups cake flour

1½ teaspoons baking powder

Pinch salt

3¼ ounces unsalted butter, room temperature

1¼ cups sugar

1 large egg

1 large egg white

3 tablespoons orange zest

1 teaspoon orange extract

1½ tablespoons poppy seeds

½ cup buttermilk

Orange Frosting (page 17)

Orange food coloring

Garnish

¼ cup poppy seeds

½ cup candied orange zest

Cupcake Cake Idea

· **10-inch serving plate**
· **Fresh orange wedges or clementines**

Place the cake in the center of the plate and arrange the cupcakes, interspersed with clementine or orange wedges, all around.

1 Preheat oven to 350°F. Line a cupcake pan with paper liners and generously grease a 6-inch round cake pan. In a medium bowl, sift together flour, baking powder and salt. In a separate bowl, beat butter and sugar at high speed until light and fluffy.

2 Reduce speed and mix in egg, egg white, orange zest, orange extract and poppy seeds.

3 Add flour mixture to butter mixture in 3 batches, alternating with buttermilk, and mixing on low speed after each addition. Beat at high speed for 1 minute until thoroughly combined.

4 Pour batter into cupcake liners and cake pan until ⅔ full. Bake the cupcakes for about 15 minutes and the cake for about 25 minutes until a toothpick inserted in the center comes out clean. Set aside to cool.

5 Frost the cupcakes and cake with frosting, and then sprinkle with poppy seeds and candied orange zest on top. Serve immediately or refrigerate for up to 2 days in an airtight container.

Love Me Do Cupcake Cake

Here's an unambiguous way of expressing your love: one giant heart cake and two dozen heart-enhanced cupcakes. Great for bringing to Valentine parties at home or school.

**Makes 24 small cupcakes and
one 11 x 9-inch heart-shaped cake**

Ingredients

Cupcakes

3 cups cake flour

3 teaspoons baking powder

Pinch salt

6½ ounces unsalted butter, room
    temperature

2 cups sugar

2 large eggs

2 large egg whites

2 teaspoons vanilla extract

1 cup buttermilk

1 cup fresh raspberries

Frosting

6 ounces unsalted butter, room
    temperature

5 cups confectioners' sugar

1 tablespoon rosewater

Pink food coloring

Red food coloring

Garnish

Heart sprinkles

Place the cake on a heart-shaped plate and place cupcakes with the 'I' 'heart' 'U' on the middle of the cake. Arrange the rest of the cupcakes in a border around the edge of the cake.

Cupcakes

1 Preheat oven to 350°F. Line a cupcake pan with paper liners and generously grease an 11 x 9-inch heart-shaped cake pan.

2 In a medium bowl, sift together flour, baking powder and salt.

3 In a separate bowl, beat butter and sugar at high speed until light and fluffy.

4 Reduce speed and mix in eggs, egg whites and vanilla extract.

5 Add flour mixture to butter mixture in 3 batches, alternating with buttermilk, and mixing on low speed after each addition. Beat at high speed for 1 minute until thoroughly combined. Fold in the raspberries.

6 Pour batter into cupcake liners and cake pan until ⅔ full. Bake the cupcakes for about 20 minutes and the cake for about 30 minutes, or until a toothpick inserted in the center comes out clean. Set aside to cool.

Frosting

7 In the bowl of an electric mixer, beat butter, confectioners' sugar and rosewater extract at high speed until light and fluffy. Tint 3 tablespoons of frosting with red food coloring, and divide the rest of the frosting evenly between two bowls. Tint one bowl of frosting with pink food coloring and leave the rest of the frosting white.

8 Pipe the letters I and U on two cupcakes, place the heart candy on a third cupcake, and decorate the rest of the cupcakes with heart sprinkles. Serve immediately or transfer to an airtight container and refrigerate for up to 2 days.

Nuts About You Cupcake Cake

This lovely light treat is an excellent way of showing your love. Top with chocolate frosting and decorate with chocolate curls for extra elegance.

Makes 6 small cupcakes and one 6-inch cake

Ingredients

Cupcakes

4 eggs, separated
½ cup sugar
½ cup self-rising flour
⅔ cup ground almonds
¾ ounce unsalted butter, room
   temperature
3 tablespoons milk
Basic Chocolate Frosting (page 16)

Garnish

Chocolate curls

1 Preheat oven to 350°F. Line a cupcake pan with paper liners and generously grease a 6-inch cake pan.

2 Place the egg whites in a large bowl and beat until stiff peaks form.

3 Slowly add sugar and continue beating until egg whites are thick and glossy. Beat in the egg yolks, one at a time, until thoroughly combined.

4 Sift the flour into the egg mixture then fold in the ground almonds.

5 Combine butter and milk in a small saucepan and heat over low heat until butter melts. Fold into almond mixture.

6 Pour batter into cupcake liners and cake pan until ⅔ full. Bake the cupcakes for about 15 minutes and the cake for about 25 minutes, or until a toothpick inserted in the center comes out clean.

7 Frost the cupcakes and cake and then sprinkle with chocolate curls. Serve immediately or refrigerate for up to 2 days in an airtight container.

Cupcake Cake Idea

· **Toothpicks***
· **Serving dish**
· **Heart candies**

Insert a toothpick through the base of each cupcake and arrange the cupcakes around the circumference of the cake. Place the cake on a serving dish and sprinkle heart candies all around.

* Remove toothpicks before serving.

Conversion Charts

The recipes that appear in this cookbook use the standard United States method for measuring liquid and dry or solid ingredients (teaspoons, tablespoons, and cups). The information on this chart is provided to help cooks outside the U.S. successfully use these recipes. All equivalents are approximate.

Metric Equivalents
For Different Types Of Ingredients

A standard cup measure of a dry or solid ingredient will vary in weight depending on the type of ingredient. A standard cup of liquid is the same volume for any type of liquid. Use the following chart when converting standard cup measures to grams (weight) or milliliters (volume).

Standard Cup		Fine Powder (ex. flour)		Grain (ex.rice)		Granular (ex. sugar)		Liquid Solids (ex. butter)		Liquid (ex. milk)
1	=	140 g	=	150 g	=	190 g	=	200 g	=	240 ml
¾	=	105 g	=	113 g	=	143 g	=	150 g	=	180 ml
⅔	=	93 g	=	100 g	=	125 g	=	133 g	=	160 ml
½	=	70 g	=	75 g	=	95 g	=	100 g	=	120 ml
⅓	=	47 g	=	50 g	=	63 g	=	67 g	=	80 ml
¼	=	35 g	=	38 g	=	48 g	=	50 g	=	60 ml
⅛	=	18 g	=	19 g	=	24 g	=	25 g	=	30 ml

Useful Equivalents
For Dry Ingredients By Weight

To convert ounces to grams, multiply the number
of oz by 30

1 oz	=	$\frac{1}{16}$ lb	=	30g
4 oz	=	¼ lb	=	120g
8 oz	=	½ lb	=	240g
12 oz	=	¾ lb	=	480g

Useful Equivalents
For Length

To convert inches to centimeters, multiply number
of inches by 2.5

1 in				2.5 cm		
6 in	=	½ ft		15 cm		
12 in	=	1 ft		30 cm		
36 in	=	3 ft	=	1 yd	90 cm	
40 in				100 cm	=	1 m

Useful Equivalents
For Cooking/Oven Temperatures

	Fahrenheit	**Celsius**		**Gas Mark**
Freeze Water	32° F	=	0° C	=	3
Room Temperature	68° F	=	20° C	=	4
Boil Water	212° F	=	100° C	=	5
Bake	325° F	=	160° C	=	6
	350° F	=	180° C	=	7
	375° F	=	190° C	=	8
	400° F	=	200° C		
	425° F		220° C		
	450° F		230° C		
Broil				Grill

Useful Equivalents
For Liquid Ingredients By Volume

¼ tsp							1 ml
½ tsp							2 ml
1 tsp	=	1 tbls					5 ml
3 tsp	=	2 tbls	=	⅛ cup	=	½ fl oz	=	15 ml
		4 tbls	=	¼ cup	=	1 fl oz	=	30 ml
		5⅓	=	⅓ cup	=	2 fl oz	=	60 ml
		8 tbls	=	½ cup	=	3 fl oz	=	80 ml
		10⅔	=	⅔ cup	=	4 fl oz	=	120 ml
		12 tbls	=	¾ cup	=	5 fl oz	=	160 ml
		16 tbls	=	1 cup	=	6 fl oz	=	180 ml
		1 pt	=	2 cups	=	8 fl oz	=	240 ml
		1 qt	=	4 cups	=	16 fl oz	=	480 ml
						32 fl oz	=	960 ml
						33 fl oz	=	1000ml

Index

DATE